OUT OF YOUR MIND

A TarcherPerigee Book

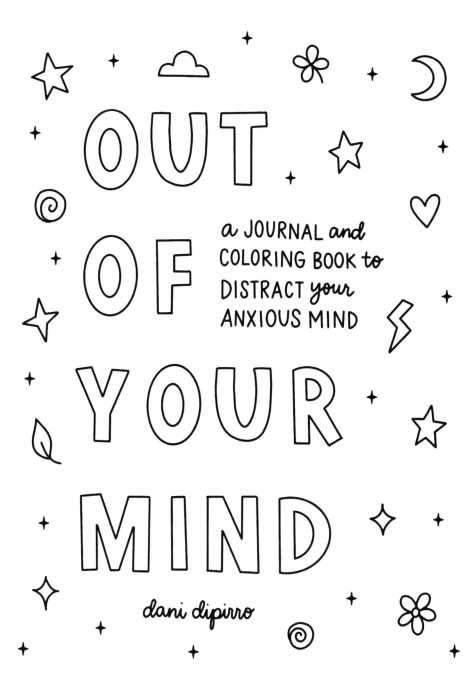

OUT OF YOUR MIND

a JOURNAL and COLORING BOOK to DISTRACT your ANXIOUS MIND

dani dipirro

tarcherperigee

an imprint of Penguin Random House LLC
penguinrandomhouse.com

Most TarcherPerigee books are available at special quantity discounts for bulk purchase
for sales promotions, premiums, fund-raising, and educational needs.
Special books or book excerpts also can be created to fit specific needs.
For details, write: SpecialMarkets@penguinrandomhouse.com.

Trade paperback ISBN: 9780593538388
Library of Congress Control Number: 2022936108

Printed in the United States of America
7th Printing

PUBLISHER'S NOTE
Neither the publisher nor the author is engaged in rendering professional advice or services to the
individual reader. The ideas, procedures, and suggestions contained in this book are not intended as
a substitute for consulting with your physician. All matters regarding your health require medical
supervision. Neither the author nor the publisher shall be liable or responsible for any loss or
damage allegedly arising from any information or suggestion in this book.

OUT OF YOUR MIND

INTRODUCTION

WELCOME TO <u>OUT OF YOUR MIND</u>! I'M DANI, AND I CREATED THIS ACTIVITY-FILLED BOOK TO PROVIDE YOU (AND ME!) WITH A POSITIVE DISTRACTION FOR YOUR ANXIOUS MIND.

FOR YEARS, I'VE CREATED ART AND SELF-HELP CONTENT FOR MY WEBSITE, POSITIVELY PRESENT, TO HELP ME COPE WITH MY ANXIETY. RECENTLY I'VE REALIZED THAT, WHILE IT'S GREAT TO SOUL-SEARCH AND LEARN ABOUT THE CAUSES OF (AND COPING MECHANISMS FOR) ANXIETY, WHAT HELPS ME THE MOST WHEN I'M IN THE THICK OF AN ANXIETY SPIRAL IS DOING SOMETHING TO GET OUT OF MY OWN HEAD. A CREATIVE DISTRACTION USUALLY WORKS BEST!

ANXIETY IS INHERENTLY CREATIVE, WHICH IS WHY AN OUTLET LIKE THIS BOOK CAN BE SO HELPFUL FOR BREAKING THE OVERTHINKING CYCLE. EVEN IF YOU DON'T FEEL LIKE YOU'RE A "CREATIVE" TYPE, THIS IS STILL THE BOOK FOR YOU. IT'S BEEN DESIGNED USING MY OWN ANXIOUS MIND TO HELP YOU CHANNEL YOUR CREATIVITY AND QUIET YOUR ANXIETY.

DISTRACTION MIGHT SOUND LIKE AVOIDANCE, AND I CERTAINLY DON'T WANT TO ENCOURAGE YOU TO AVOID FEELINGS. FEELINGS SHOULD BE FELT! BUT, AS ANYONE WITH ANXIETY KNOWS, SOMETIMES YOU NEED A BREAK FROM THE FEELINGS. SOMETIMES DIVING INTO A SOUL-SEARCHING BOOK OR JOURNAL ISN'T WHAT YOUR ANXIOUS MIND NEEDS.

THIS BOOK IS FOR THOSE MOMENTS WHEN YOU FEEL YOU CAN'T DO ANYTHING, BUT YOU KNOW DOING SOMETHING TO COMPLETELY NUMB YOUR MIND ISN'T THE BEST SOLUTION. DISTRACTION IS POWERFUL, BUT IT TAKES THE RIGHT KIND OF DISTRACTION TO STOP YOU FROM DWELLING ON WORRIED THOUGHTS. I'VE DESIGNED THESE PAGES TO BE JUST THE RIGHT AMOUNT OF DISTRACTION—SIMPLE ACTIVITIES WITH ENOUGH DEPTH TO BE MEANINGFUL.

BY CHANNELING YOUR CREATIVITY INTO THIS BOOK, YOU CAN DISRUPT OVER-THINKING, EMBRACE IMAGINATIVE EXPRESSION, EXPLORE YOUR EMOTIONS IN NEW WAYS, AND MAYBE EVEN DEFUSE SOME OF YOUR ANXIETY.

THIS BOOK CAN BE USED IN ANY ORDER. SOME PAGES ARE COMPLETELY ABOUT MINDLESS DISTRACTION—SIMPLE EXERCISES OR COLORING PAGES—WHILE OTHERS DIG A LITTLE DEEPER. CHOOSE WHAT WORKS BEST FOR YOUR CURRENT EMOTIONAL STATE. IF YOU TURN TO A PAGE AND IT FEELS LIKE IT'S ADDING TO YOUR ANXIETY, FLIP TO ANOTHER ONE.

BECAUSE THE ACT OF COLORING HAS BEEN KNOWN TO HELP QUELL ANXIETY, MOST OF THE PAGES CAN BE COLORED IN, EVEN IF THAT'S NOT THEIR INITIAL PURPOSE, WHICH PROVIDES A BONUS CREATIVE OUTLET!

AS YOU WORK THROUGH THESE PAGES, REMEMBER: YOU DON'T HAVE TO BE "GOOD" AT ANY OF THESE THINGS. YOU DON'T HAVE TO ACE THE ACTIVITIES OR HAVE STELLAR SCRIBBLING SKILLS TO BENEFIT FROM THIS BOOK.

THESE PAGES ARE LIKELY TO HELP YOU INTERRUPT YOUR RUMINATION, FOCUS MORE ON THE PRESENT MOMENT, INCREASE YOUR SELF-ESTEEM THROUGH CREATIVITY, REDUCE OVERSTIMULATION, EXPERIENCE PLAYFULNESS, FEEL LESS STRESSED, AND MAYBE EVEN LEARN A THING OR TWO ABOUT YOURSELF! I'M NOT SAYING THIS BOOK IS GOING TO CHANGE YOUR LIFE…BUT IT JUST MIGHT IF YOU LET IT.

NOW, LET'S SEE WHAT HAPPENS IF YOU GET OUT OF YOUR MIND FOR A BIT…

FIND ADDITIONAL RESOURCES FOR ANXIETY ON POSITIVELYPRESENT.COM, INCLUDING: CURATED SPOTIFY PLAYLISTS BASED ON VARIOUS MOODS (TO HELP YOU FIND THE PERFECT VIBE WHILE YOU'RE WORKING ON THESE PAGES!), AN ANXIETY-RELATED RECOMMENDED READING LIST, AND MORE!

ANXIETY-FIGHTING ACTIVITIES

DIFFERENT ACTIVITIES HELP US QUELL ANXIETY. CIRCLE THE
ONES BELOW THAT WORK BEST FOR YOU AND TRY TO
INCORPORATE AT LEAST ONE INTO YOUR DAILY ROUTINE.

TAKE A
NAP

MOVE YOUR
BODY

COLOR OR
DRAW

GO OUTSIDE

GET COZY

PRACTICE
GRATITUDE

CREATE A
CRAFT

WATCH YOUR
FAVORITE FILM

DO SOMETHING
SOOTHING

LISTEN TO MUSIC

READ A
GOOD BOOK

WRITE YOUR
FEELINGS

TRY A
BREATHING
EXERCISE

TAKE A DAY OFF

PLAY A GAME

TEXT A
POSITIVE PAL

CONNECT WITH
OTHERS

SEEK OUT
INSPIRING STORIES

HELP SOMEONE
IN NEED

NOTICE WHAT'S
GOING WELL

SOOTHING SOUNDS

WRITE THE NAMES OF SONGS (OR SOUNDS!) THAT HELP SOOTHE
YOU WHEN YOU'RE FEELING STRESSED. COLOR IN THE TAPES
USING COLORS THAT COMPLEMENT THE SONGS. IF POSSIBLE,
MAKE A PLAYLIST TO LISTEN TO WHEN YOU'RE ANXIOUS.

FIND GOOD FEELINGS

MAYBE THE WORDS YOU NEED TO SEE ARE IN THE WORD SEARCH BELOW! BUT EVEN IF THEY'RE NOT, DOING AN ACTIVITY LIKE THIS CAN BE A GREAT DISTRACTION WHEN YOU'RE ANXIOUS.

```
Y  V  M  O  D  S  I  W  C  A  N  D  O  M  P
Z  P  U  R  P  O  S  E  P  H  O  C  L  M  I
F  Y  I  W  N  O  Q  J  S  Q  I  O  U  Z  H
O  F  T  L  E  V  A  R  T  E  T  U  A  Q  S
R  Y  T  I  V  I  T  A  E  R  C  R  X  U  D
G  W  B  R  N  O  P  Q  V  U  E  A  Y  Y  N
I  C  N  N  E  U  S  N  O  S  N  G  J  Q  E
V  N  H  M  O  S  T  U  L  O  N  E  P  T  I
E  L  A  A  E  I  T  R  E  L  O  D  U  T  R
N  F  J  C  N  S  S  A  O  C  C  G  R  E  F
E  Y  C  S  L  G  B  S  M  P  A  O  H  N  O
S  U  V  M  K  L  E  H  A  I  P  E  G  E  C
S  H  T  L  A  E  H  A  T  P  N  O  P  R  U
J  O  W  E  A  L  T  H  U  U  U  A  N  G  S
P  G  R  O  W  T  H  S  F  A  M  I  L  Y  K
```

WISDOM	PURPOSE	GROWTH	FORGIVENESS	COURAGE
ENERGY	FOCUS	SUCCESS	HEALTH	PEACE
PASSION	STAMINA	CREATIVITY	SUPPORT	FRIENDSHIP
CHANGE	CLOSURE	LOVE	OPPORTUNITY	CONNECTION

ANSWER KEY AT THE END OF THE BOOK!

PLANT IT TO PLAN IT!

MAKING PLANS MIGHT NOT BE ON THE AGENDA RIGHT NOW,
BUT THOUGHTS CAN BECOME THINGS! ON THE PLANTS,
WRITE THE EMOTIONS YOU'D LIKE TO EXPERIENCE
WHEN YOU'RE FEELING LESS ANXIOUS.

SENSORY SCAVENGER HUNT

CONNECTING WITH YOUR SENSES IS ONE OF THE BEST WAYS TO
BRING YOURSELF BACK TO THE PRESENT. TRY IT BY WRITING...

5 THINGS YOU CAN SEE

_____

_____

_____

_____

_____

4 THINGS YOU CAN TOUCH

_____

_____

_____

3 THINGS YOU CAN HEAR

_____

_____

2 THINGS YOU CAN SMELL

_____

1 THING YOU CAN TASTE

_____

NOTE TO SELF

WRITE A COMPASSIONATE LETTER TO YOURSELF, AS IF
YOU WERE WRITING TO A LOVED ONE. WHAT KIND
WORDS WOULD YOU SAY TO SOMEONE WHO'S
FEELING HOW YOU'RE FEELING RIGHT NOW?

CIRCLE OF CONTROL

IN THE OUTER CIRCLE, WRITE DOWN WHAT YOU HAD NO
CONTROL OVER TODAY (OTHER PEOPLE, WEATHER, ETC.). IN THE
INNER CIRCLE, WRITE DOWN THINGS THAT WERE WITHIN YOUR
CONTROL (YOUR ATTITUDE, REACTIONS, ETC.).

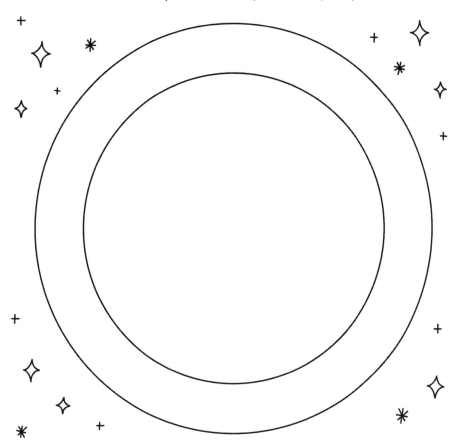

WHAT'S IN THE INNER CIRCLE CAN BE VERY POWERFUL! USE THIS
PAGE AS A REMINDER TO FOCUS YOUR ATTENTION ON WHAT YOU
CAN CONTROL RATHER THAN WORRYING ABOUT WHAT YOU CAN'T.

SEARCH AND FIND

FIND ALL OF THE STARS IN THE SEA OF SHAPES BELOW
AND COLOR THEM IN. BONUS ACTIVITY: CHOOSE A COLOR
FOR EACH SHAPE AND COLOR EACH ONE IN.

ANSWER KEY AT THE END OF THE BOOK!

WHEEL OF EMOTIONS

MINDFULLY COLOR IN EACH SECTION WITH A COLOR YOU ASSOCIATE WITH THAT EMOTION. IF YOU'RE EVER UNSURE, COME BACK TO THIS PAGE TO SEE WHICH COLOR RESONATES.

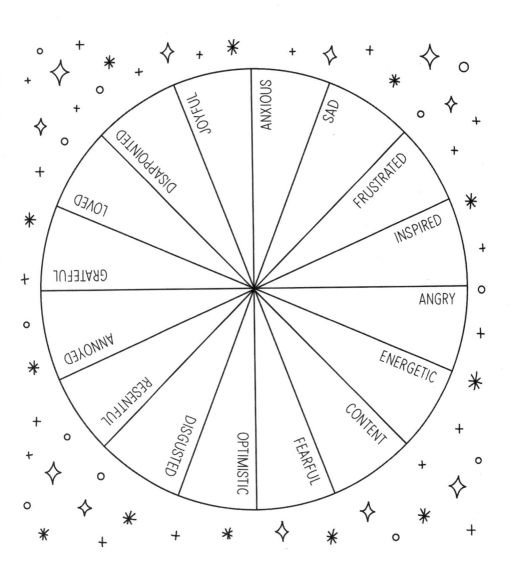

YOU MIGHT NOT
HAVE HAD THE MOST
PRODUCTIVE DAY TODAY,
BUT SOMETIMES WE
BEHAVE DIFFERENTLY
WHEN WE'RE ANXIOUS.

TRY NOT TO BE SO
HARD ON YOURSELF.
YOU'RE DOING THE
BEST YOU CAN.

STRESS-RELIEVING SPELL

IF YOU COULD MAKE YOUR OWN STRESS-RELIEF POTION, WHICH
INGREDIENTS WOULD YOU PUT IN THE POT? COLOR THOSE IN
(OR COLOR THEM ALL AND CIRCLE YOUR TOP THREE!).

BELOW THE SURFACE

IN THE PART OF THE ICEBERG THAT'S ABOVE THE WATER, WRITE DOWN WHAT OTHERS MIGHT KNOW ABOUT HOW YOU'RE FEELING. IN THE UNDERWATER AREA, WRITE DOWN ALL THE THOUGHTS AND FEELINGS OTHERS CAN'T SEE.

BE YOUR OWN BEST FRIEND

YOU MIGHT NOT BE VERY KIND TO YOURSELF WHEN YOU'RE ANXIOUS, BUT YOU'RE PROBABLY KIND TO YOUR ANXIOUS FRIENDS. USE THE CHART BELOW TO PRACTICE BEING KINDER TO YOUR ANXIOUS THOUGHTS.

IF MY FRIEND SAID...	I WOULD SAY...
I can't do anything right! I'm a total failure, and I will never be able to accomplish anything because I'm always so anxious.	That's not true! You are just having a rough time right now and that makes it hard to remember all that you've accomplished.

SOUND THE ALARM!

ON THESE CLOCKS, WRITE THE SIGNALS YOUR BODY SENDS YOU
WHEN YOU'RE FEELING ANXIOUS, LIKE "FASTER HEARTBEAT,"
"SWEATING," "FOGGY BRAIN," ETC. KNOWING YOUR BODY'S ALARMS
CAN HELP YOU PREPARE THE NEXT TIME ANXIETY STRIKES!

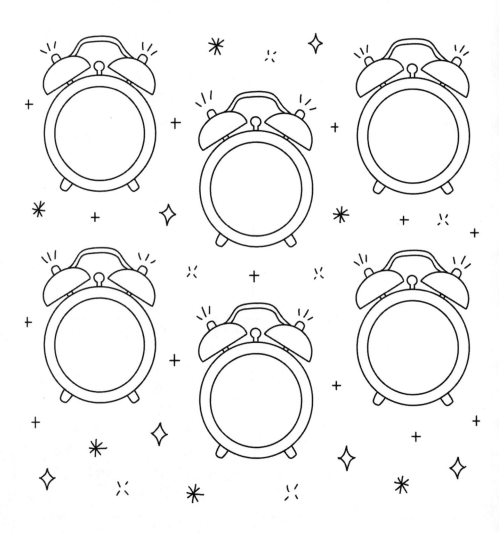

ENERGY ASSESSMENT

LIST THINGS—PEOPLE, EXPERIENCES, THOUGHTS, ETC.—THAT
GIVE OR TAKE ENERGY FROM YOU. TRY TO INCORPORATE
AT LEAST ONE ENERGY-GIVER INTO YOUR LIFE TODAY
(AND TRY TO AVOID THE ENERGY-TAKERS WHEN YOU CAN)!

ENERGY-GIVERS	ENERGY-TAKERS

COMPLIMENTS COLLAGE

IN EACH AREA OF THE HEART, WRITE A COMPLIMENT OR
ENCOURAGING STATEMENT TO YOURSELF. FOR EXAMPLE, "I'M SO
IMPRESSED WITH HOW WELL YOU'VE HANDLED TODAY," OR "YOU
SHOULD BE PROUD OF HOW FAR YOU'VE COME!"

THE GRATITUDE ABC'S

GRATITUDE CAN REALLY HELP WHEN YOU'RE FEELING
OVERWHELMED. WRITE SOMETHING YOU'RE THANKFUL FOR
BEGINNING WITH EACH LETTER OF THE ALPHABET.

A _____

B _____

C _____

D _____

E _____

F _____

G _____

H _____

I _____

J _____

K _____

L _____

M _____

N _____

O _____

P _____

Q _____

R _____

S _____

T _____

U _____

V _____

W _____

X _____

Y _____

Z _____

MAKE YOUR WISHES

IT MIGHT BE DIFFICULT TO IMAGINE A POSITIVE FUTURE RIGHT NOW, BUT GOOD THINGS WILL HAPPEN. MAKE A WISH ON EACH STAR BELOW AND, AS YOU COLOR IN THE STAR'S PATTERN, TRY TO IMAGINE HOW IT WILL FEEL TO HAVE THAT WISH COME TRUE.

MIX AND MATCH MOTTO

PICK PHRASES FROM THE TWO COLUMNS BELOW TO CREATE
A MOTTO THAT HELPS YOU FEEL LESS ANXIOUS. AFTER
YOU'VE CHOSEN WHAT YOU LIKE BEST, WRITE IT
THREE TIMES TO CEMENT IT INTO YOUR MIND.

TODAY I CHOOSE	OPTIMISM
TODAY I'LL TAKE NOTICE OF	HOPE
TODAY I EMBRACE	GROWTH
TODAY I WILL FOCUS ON	KINDNESS
TODAY I'LL SEEK OUT	JOY
TODAY I WILL CREATE	WISDOM
TODAY I WELCOME	INSPIRATION
TODAY I'LL EMBODY	STRENGTH
TODAY I WILL ENCOUNTER	CALM

_____

_____

_____

YOU ARE NOT ANXIOUS.
YOU ARE <u>FEELING</u> ANXIOUS.

AND FEELINGS
AREN'T FACTS.

YOU ARE MORE THAN
WHATEVER YOU'RE FEELING
IN THIS MOMENT.

CARDS YOU'RE DEALT

SOME DAYS YOU'RE DEALT A GOOD HAND AND OTHER DAYS
NOT SO MUCH. ON THE CARDS BELOW, WRITE ABOUT
CIRCUMSTANCES OUTSIDE OF YOUR CONTROL AND
HOW THEY'RE IMPACTING YOUR MOOD TODAY.

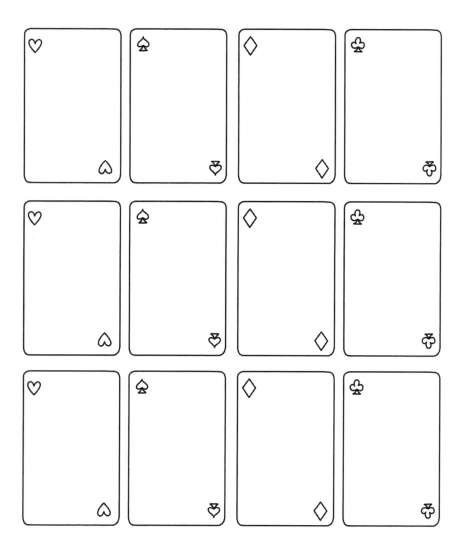

WINDOW OF REFLECTION

STAYING IN THE MOMENT CAN BE SO HARD WHEN YOU'RE
ANXIOUS, SO TAKE A BREAK FROM YOUR THOUGHTS RIGHT NOW
AND FIND A WINDOW NEARBY. LOOK OUT THE WINDOW AND
LIST (OR DRAW!) EVERYTHING YOU SEE IN THE FRAME.

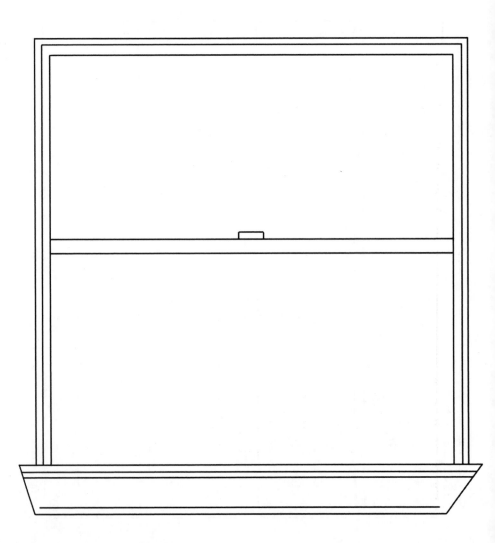

TO-DONE LIST

LIST EVERYTHING YOU'VE DONE TODAY (EVEN THE TINIEST THINGS!). WHEN YOU'RE ANXIOUS, YOU MIGHT FEEL AS IF YOU'VE DONE NOTHING AT ALL, BUT YOU'VE LIKELY ACCOMPLISHED MORE THAN YOU REALIZE.

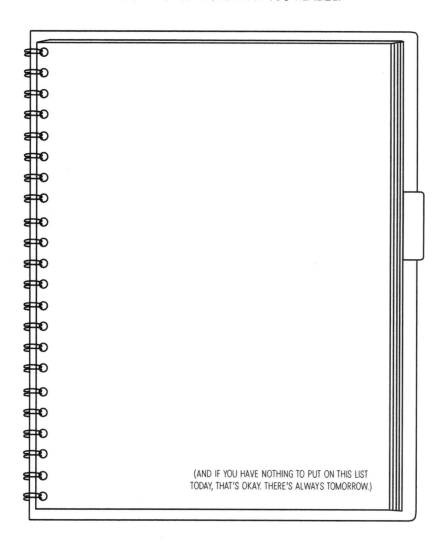

(AND IF YOU HAVE NOTHING TO PUT ON THIS LIST TODAY, THAT'S OKAY. THERE'S ALWAYS TOMORROW.)

PROTEST YOUR ANXIETY

JUST BECAUSE ANXIOUS THOUGHTS HAVE FOUND THEIR WAY
INTO YOUR MIND, THAT DOESN'T MEAN YOU HAVE TO TOLERATE
THEIR PRESENCE. ON THE SIGNS BELOW, WRITE WHAT YOU
WOULD SAY TO YOUR ANXIETY IF YOU COULD PROTEST IT.

BE (VICARIOUSLY) JOYFUL

FEELING JOYFUL IN THE MIDST OF ANXIETY ISN'T EASY. INSTEAD OF FEELING PRESSURE TO FIND YOUR OWN JOY, USE THIS PAGE TO CELEBRATE THE JOY OF OTHERS. WHAT WONDERFUL THINGS HAVE HAPPENED TO PEOPLE YOU KNOW LATELY?

ANXIETY-FREE APOTHECARY

WELCOME TO THE ANXIETY-FREE APOTHECARY! TAKE A BREAK
FROM YOUR WORRIES AND COLOR IN THE BOTTLES BELOW,
STARTING WITH THE ONES YOU'D BE MOST LIKELY TO
PURCHASE IF THEY EXISTED IN REAL LIFE!

THIS OR THAT?

WHEN IT COMES TO SELF-CARE, WHAT WORKS FOR ONE PERSON MIGHT NOT WORK FOR ANOTHER. TAKE A LOOK AT THE CHOICES BELOW AND CIRCLE THE MOST APPEALING OPTION.
DO ONE OF THEM TODAY IF YOU CAN!

TAKE A
BUBBLE BATH

GO FOR A
LONG WALK

WATCH A FAVORITE
FILM SOLO

PLAY A GAME
WITH FRIENDS

START A NEW
CREATIVE PROJECT

WRITE ABOUT HOW
YOU'RE FEELING

READ A
GOOD BOOK

GET YOUR
BODY MOVING

DIY DANDELION

DOING SOMETHING YOU'VE NEVER DONE BEFORE CAN REALLY
BOOST YOUR CONFIDENCE AND REDUCE ANXIETY. USE THE STEP-
BY-STEP TUTORIAL TO DRAW A DANDELION. WHEN
YOU'RE FINISHED, MAKE A WISH ON IT!

STEP ONE: DRAW A LINE WITH
AN ASTERISK ON THE END

STEP TWO: ADD LEAVES TO THE
SIDES OF THE LINE

STEP THREE: DRAW LOTS OF
ASTERISKS IN A CIRCLE

STEP FOUR: ADD PLUS SIGNS AND
DOTS TO FILL IN THE SPACES

SPILL YOUR SECRETS

IT CAN BE HARD TO WRITE ABOUT HOW YOU FEEL. TO MAKE IT
EASIER (AND MORE FUN!), WRITE ABOUT WHAT YOU'RE FEELING
RIGHT NOW USING THE SECRET LANGUAGE BELOW. (FOR EXTRA
SECRECY, RIP OFF THE BOTTOM OF THE PAGE AND HIDE IT!)

A◎ B✳ C+ D↗ Em F◎ G⌀ H≡ I◈ J♡ K△ L✗✗ M◖
N⋈ O# P△ Q✕ R⊶ S□ T✩ U⌒ V◔ W✯ X℥ Y⊗ Z✦

IT WILL BE OKAY.
MAYBE NOT TODAY.
MAYBE NOT EVEN
TOMORROW. BUT
SOMEDAY SOON
IT WILL BE.
KEEP GOING.

DAILY DELIGHTS

FOCUSING ON THE LITTLE POSITIVE THINGS CAN BE A
WONDERFUL DISTRACTION FROM ANXIOUS THOUGHTS. ON THE
LEFT, YOU'LL FIND A LIST OF DELIGHTFUL THINGS. USE THEM TO
INSPIRE YOU TO CREATE YOUR OWN LIST ON THE RIGHT.

THE SUN COMING OUT AFTER A CLOUDY DAY _____

HEARING A FAVORITE SONG UNEXPECTEDLY _____

QUOTES EXPRESSING FEELINGS SO WELL _____

LAUGHING HARD AT SOMETHING SILLY _____

THE VICARIOUS JOY FOR OTHERS' WINS _____

TRYING SOMETHING NEW AND ENJOYING IT _____

SIGNS OF A NEW SEASON BEGINNING _____

WATCHING SOMETHING THAT WARMS YOUR HEART _____

THE VOICE OF SOMEONE YOU LOVE _____

SEEING ART THAT SPEAKS TO YOUR SOUL _____

AN ALBUM WITH ABSOLUTELY ZERO SKIPS _____

FINISHING A CHORE YOU'D BEEN AVOIDING _____

RECEIVING A KIND COMPLIMENT _____

SONG LYRIC THERAPY

THE LYRICS YOU LISTEN TO CAN BE POWERFUL. CHOOSE A SONG
THAT'S REALLY SPEAKING TO YOU RIGHT NOW AND WRITE
THE MOST RELATABLE LYRICS BELOW.

WOULD YOU RATHER?

TAKE A BREAK FROM HEAVY THINKING AND HAVE SOME FUN
(AND MAYBE LEARN SOMETHING ABOUT YOURSELF!) WITH
THIS QUICK Q&A. CIRCLE YOUR FAVORITES!

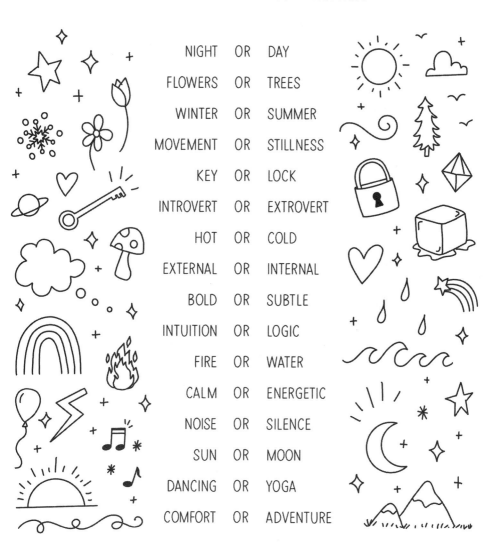

NIGHT	OR	DAY
FLOWERS	OR	TREES
WINTER	OR	SUMMER
MOVEMENT	OR	STILLNESS
KEY	OR	LOCK
INTROVERT	OR	EXTROVERT
HOT	OR	COLD
EXTERNAL	OR	INTERNAL
BOLD	OR	SUBTLE
INTUITION	OR	LOGIC
FIRE	OR	WATER
CALM	OR	ENERGETIC
NOISE	OR	SILENCE
SUN	OR	MOON
DANCING	OR	YOGA
COMFORT	OR	ADVENTURE

BREATHE IN, BREATHE OUT

TRACE EACH OF THE SHAPES BELOW. THE FIRST TIME,
BREATHE IN. THE SECOND TIME, BREATHE OUT. REPEAT
AS OFTEN AS YOU NEED TO TO CREATE CALM.

GET TO KNOW YOURSELF

IN THE MIDST OF ANXIETY, YOU MIGHT FEEL DISCONNECTED
FROM YOURSELF. GET BACK IN TOUCH WITH WHO YOU ARE
BY ANSWERING THE QUESTIONS BELOW.

IF I COULD LIVE ANYWHERE, I'D LIVE… _____

I WOULD LOVE TO LET GO OF… _____

IF I WERE A COLOR, I WOULD BE… _____

I FEEL MOST ALIVE WHEN I AM… _____

I COULD NEVER PUT A PRICE ON… _____

SOMEDAY I HOPE I AM ABLE TO… _____

I AM HAPPIEST WHEN I AM… _____

SO FAR, THIS YEAR HAS BEEN… _____

I TEND TO STRUGGLE WITH… _____

THE MOTTO I TRY TO LIVE BY IS… _____

IF I COULD BE AN ANIMAL, I'D BE… _____

MY LIFE IS BETTER WHEN I… _____

SOMETIMES I PRETEND TO BE… _____

BURST YOUR BUBBLE

IN THE SMALL BUBBLES, WRITE AN ANXIOUS THOUGHT YOU'RE HAVING, LIKE "I'M GOING TO FAIL MY PRESENTATION." IN THE LARGE BUBBLES, CHALLENGE THE THOUGHT WITH SOMETHING LIKE, "I AM PREPARED AND UNLIKELY TO FAIL. BUT EVEN IF I DO END UP FAILING, I'LL STILL BE OKAY. I AM STRONG."

PERMISSION GRANTED

SOMETIMES YOU HAVE TO GIVE YOURSELF PERMISSION TO TAKE A TIME-OUT. FILL OUT THE PERMISSION SLIP WITH WHATEVER YOU NEED TO ALLOW YOURSELF TO DO TODAY—RELAX, AVOID OVERTHINKING, REST, STEP AWAY FROM YOUR TO-DO LIST, ETC.

I, _____ (NAME), GIVE MYSELF PERMISSION TO DO THE FOLLOWING ACTIVITY, _____ (ACTIVITY), WITHOUT HESITATION OR GUILT TODAY. BY SIGNING BELOW, I GRANT MYSELF THE FOLLOWING:

1. THE RIGHT TO DO THE ACTIVITY LISTED ABOVE
2. THE RIGHT TO NOT FEEL GUILTY ABOUT TAKING CARE OF MYSELF
3. THE RIGHT TO RETURN TO THIS ACTIVITY AS OFTEN AS I LIKE
4. THE RIGHT TO REQUEST HELP FROM OTHERS (IF NEEDED)

I GRANT MYSELF PERMISSION TO DO ALL OF THE ABOVE WITHOUT JUDGMENT OR WORRY.

_____   _____
(SIGNATURE)   (DATE)

THE PRIORITIES PYRAMID

USE THE PYRAMID TO CREATE A HIERARCHY OF YOUR CURRENT
PRIORITIES, WITH THE MOST IMPORTANT AT THE BOTTOM OF THE
PYRAMID. GIVE YOUR ATTENTION TO THOSE FOUNDATIONAL
PRIORITIES TODAY AND WORRY LESS ABOUT THOSE AT THE TOP.

IDEAL EMOTIONS

IF YOU COULD CHOOSE TO FEEL ANYTHING RIGHT NOW, WHAT WOULD YOU PICK? CIRCLE THE WORDS YOU'D LIKE TO FEEL AND WRITE YOUR TOP TWO IN THE BOXES BELOW. TRY TO SEEK OUT SOMETHING THAT WILL GIVE YOU THOSE FEELINGS TODAY.

CONFIDENT	JOYFUL	MOTIVATED
HOPEFUL	ENERGIZED	DREAMY
SUCCESSFUL	CREATIVE	SAFE
PLAYFUL	TRANQUIL	VICTORIOUS
EXCITED	ADVENTUROUS	HEALED
CHEERFUL	ENTHUSIASTIC	APPRECIATED
PRODUCTIVE	PREPARED	DELIGHTED
ACCEPTED	COMFORTABLE	SERENE
UNBOTHERED	INSPIRED	AMBITIOUS
BOLD	OPTIMISTIC	RELAXED
ENGAGED	MINDFUL	UNSTOPPABLE
HAPPY	UPBEAT	WISE
GENEROUS	COURAGEOUS	DECISIVE
ELATED	STRONG	EMPOWERED
CURIOUS	ACCEPTING	LIBERATED
PATIENT	CONTENT	PEACEFUL
SKILLFUL	LOVED	MAGICAL
IMAGINATIVE	TRUSTING	FEARLESS
AUTHENTIC	RESTED	JUBILANT
SECURE	CONNECTED	PASSIONATE
LOVING	GRATEFUL	SATISFIED

WHAT'S BUGGING YOU?

WHAT'S BOTHERING YOU RIGHT NOW? ASSIGN YOUR STRESSORS
TO EACH OF THE INSECTS BELOW. AS YOU COLOR THEM IN,
IMAGINE BRUSHING THOSE WORRIES AWAY FROM YOU,
JUST AS YOU WOULD A BOTHERSOME BUG.

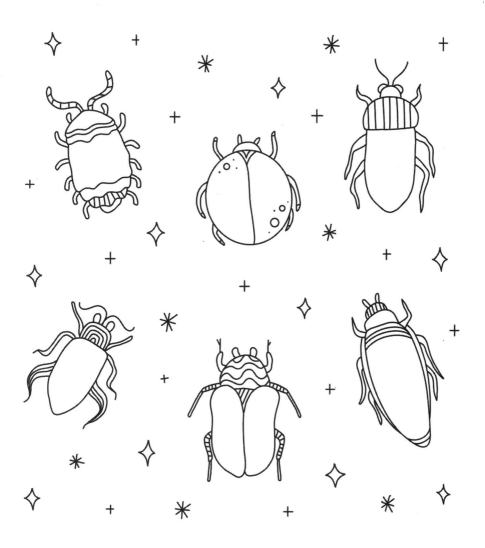

MAP YOUR PROGRESS

USE THE MAP BELOW TO EITHER: (1) EXPLORE HOW YOU'RE
GOING TO GET FROM WHERE YOU ARE TO WHERE YOU WANT TO
BE, OR (2) REFLECT ON HOW FAR YOU'VE COME SO FAR.

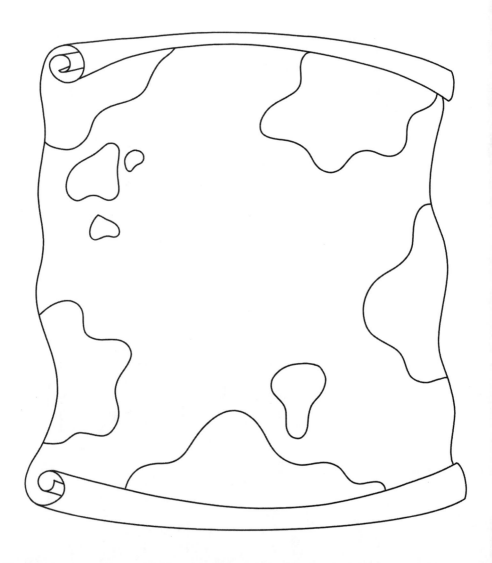

... AND THAT'S OKAY

YOU'RE PROBABLY FEELING A LOT OF THINGS RIGHT NOW, AND
THAT CAN BE OVERWHELMING. WRITE DOWN YOUR CURRENT
EMOTIONS AND REMIND YOURSELF THAT IT'S OKAY TO FEEL.

I AM FEELING _____ AND THAT'S OKAY.

I AM FEELING _____ AND THAT'S OKAY.

I AM FEELING _____ AND THAT'S OKAY.

I AM FEELING _____ AND THAT'S OKAY.

I AM FEELING _____ AND THAT'S OKAY.

I AM FEELING _____ AND THAT'S OKAY.

I AM FEELING _____ AND THAT'S OKAY.

I AM FEELING _____ AND THAT'S OKAY.

I AM FEELING _____ AND THAT'S OKAY.

I AM FEELING _____ AND THAT'S OKAY.

I AM FEELING _____ AND THAT'S OKAY.

I AM FEELING _____ AND THAT'S OKAY.

WORDS OF WISDOM

IN THE BOX BELOW, WRITE YOUR FAVORITE QUOTE OR ONE
YOU'VE READ RECENTLY THAT INSPIRED YOU. IF YOU NEED IDEAS,
CHECK OUT @POSITIVELYPRESENT ON INSTAGRAM!

FUTURE FUN

IT MIGHT NOT SEEM LIKE IT IN THIS MOMENT, BUT THIS ANXIETY
WON'T LAST FOREVER. WRITE ABOUT THE THINGS YOU'D LIKE TO
DO IN THE FUTURE WHEN YOU'RE FEELING LESS ANXIOUS.

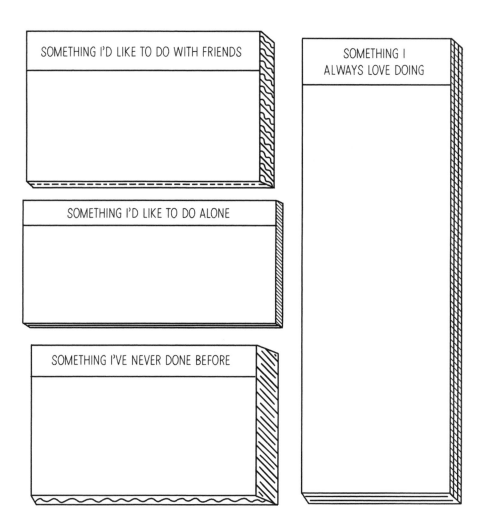

SOMETHING I'D LIKE TO DO WITH FRIENDS

SOMETHING I
ALWAYS LOVE DOING

SOMETHING I'D LIKE TO DO ALONE

SOMETHING I'VE NEVER DONE BEFORE

COLOR OF CALM

WHAT COLOR SOOTHES YOU WHENEVER YOU SEE IT? USE THAT
COLOR TO FILL IN EVERYTHING ON THIS PAGE. THE NEXT TIME
YOU'RE SUPER ANXIOUS, LOOK FOR THAT COLOR AROUND YOU
(OR COME BACK TO THIS PAGE IF YOU CAN'T FIND ANYTHING!).

A FEW FAVORITE THINGS

TAKING TIME TO REFLECT ON WHAT YOU LOVE IS A GREAT WAY
TO COUNTERACT ANXIETY. WRITE DOWN YOUR FAVORITES,
AND USE THIS PAGE AS A REMINDER TO CONNECT WITH
WHAT BRINGS YOU JOY AS OFTEN AS YOU CAN.

MY FAVORITE BOOK IS. . . _____

MY FAVORITE MEMORY IS. . . _____

MY FAVORITE COLOR IS. . . _____

MY FAVORITE ANIMAL IS. . . _____

MY FAVORITE SNACK FOOD IS. . . _____

MY FAVORITE MOVIE IS. . . _____

MY FAVORITE WEATHER IS. . . _____

MY FAVORITE SONG IS. . . _____

MY FAVORITE QUOTE IS. . . _____

MY FAVORITE PLACE IS. . . _____

MY FAVORITE OUTFIT IS. . . _____

MY FAVORITE TIME OF DAY IS. . . _____

MY FAVORITE SEASON IS. . . _____

TAKE WHAT YOU NEED

COLOR IN WHAT YOU'D LIKE MORE OF IN YOUR LIFE. CONSIDER
IF THERE'S ANY POSSIBLE WAY TO BRING THOSE FEELINGS
INTO YOUR WORLD TODAY (OR SOON, IF TODAY'S ROUGH).

FEELING HALFHEARTED

SOMETIMES HALFHEARTED EFFORT IS ALL YOU CAN OFFER
WHEN YOU'RE FEELING ANXIOUS. WHILE FILLING IN THE MISSING
HALF OF THE DRAWINGS BELOW, REMIND YOURSELF THAT IT'S
OKAY IF YOU CAN'T PUT YOUR WHOLE HEART INTO IT RIGHT NOW.

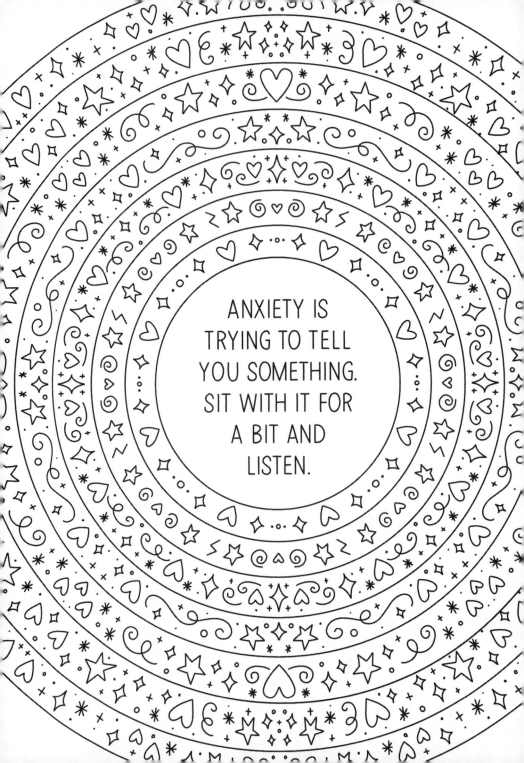

ANXIETY IS
TRYING TO TELL
YOU SOMETHING.
SIT WITH IT FOR
A BIT AND
LISTEN.

PICK A PLACE

WHICH OF THESE PLACES DO YOU FIND THE MOST SOOTHING?
COLOR THAT ONE IN WHILE IMAGINING (IN AS MUCH DETAIL AS
POSSIBLE!) WHAT IT WOULD BE LIKE TO BE THERE.

ILLUMINATE A PROBLEM

WRITE A PROBLEM YOU'RE DEALING WITH IN THE CENTER, AND
LIST ANY POSSIBLE SOLUTIONS YOU CAN THINK OF ON THE RAYS.
EVEN IF YOU CAN'T TAKE ACTION NOW, IT CAN BE HELPFUL
TO WRITE DOWN POSITIVE POSSIBILITIES.

BOOK SHELFIE

IF THIS BOOKSHELF CONTAINED STORIES OF YOUR LIFE, WHAT
WOULD THE TITLES SAY? WRITE EXPERIENCES YOU'VE HAD
SO FAR ON THE BOOK SPINES, APPRECIATING ALL THE
HIGHS AND LOWS YOU'VE LIVED THROUGH ALREADY.

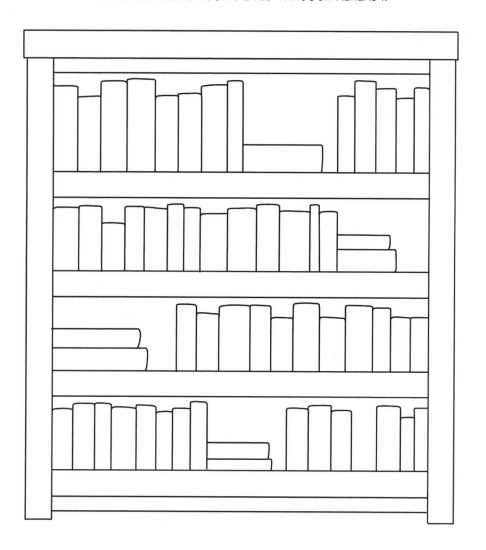

CHECK YOUR LENSES

YOUR LIFE IS IMPACTED BY THE LENSES YOU LOOK THROUGH.
ON THE LINES BELOW, IDENTIFY YOUR CURRENT PERSPECTIVE
IN THOSE AREAS OF LIFE AND CONSIDER HOW THEY MIGHT
BE INFLUENCING THE WAY YOU SEE THE WORLD.

ENVIRONMENT

MEDIA INTAKE

CURRENT MOOD

BELIEFS

EXPERIENCES

CULTURE

MIND-SET

TIME PERIOD

GRATITUDE BREAK!

IS PRACTICING GRATITUDE A CLICHÉ SELF-HELP ACTIVITY?
PERHAPS. BUT DOES IT TRULY HELP WITH ANXIETY?
DEFINITELY! WRITE DOWN 10 THINGS YOU'RE
THANKFUL FOR IN THIS MOMENT.

today i am thankful for...

1.
2.
3.
4.
5.
6.
7.
8.
9.
10.

FRAME THE FEELING

ON THE SIGNS NEXT TO EACH FRAME, WRITE A FEELING YOU'RE EXPERIENCING. INSIDE THE FRAME, DRAW (OR JUST SCRIBBLE WILDLY!) HOW THAT FEELING FEELS IN YOUR MIND AND BODY.

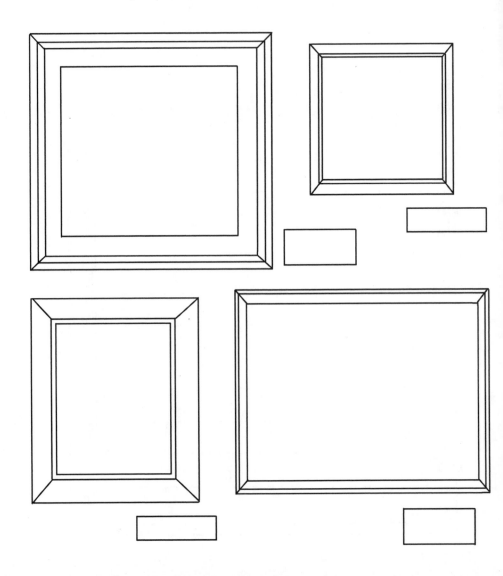

NOTICE GOOD NEWS

READING OR WATCHING NEWS STORIES CAN AMPLIFY ANXIETY,
BUT THE NEWS ISN'T ALL BAD. GO SEEK OUT SOME OPTIMISTIC
HEADLINES AND WRITE ABOUT (OR ILLUSTRATE!) THEM
ON THE NEWSPAPER BELOW.

TODAY'S DATE: ISSUE NO. 1

GOOD NEWS

PATTERNS PRACTICE

GETTING BACK TO THE MOMENT IS VITAL FOR COMBATING
ANXIETY. RETURN TO THE PRESENT BY COPYING THE
PATTERNS BELOW. TAKE YOUR TIME AND JUST BE HERE.

SELECT YOUR SEASON

EVERYONE GOES THROUGH VARIOUS SEASONS IN LIFE. COLOR IN THE ONE THAT RESONATES WITH WHERE YOU ARE RIGHT NOW. AND REMEMBER, NO MATTER WHAT SEASON YOU CURRENTLY FIND YOURSELF IN, IT WON'T LAST FOREVER.

SPRING

PERSONAL GROWTH
FRESH, NEW IDEAS
RESTLESS EXCITEMENT
OVERWHELMING ENERGY

SUMMER

EAGERNESS TO CREATE
NEWFOUND FREEDOM
BRAVE EXPLORATION
FLOURISHING GROWTH

AUTUMN

DIFFICULT TRANSFORMATION
GROWING GRATITUDE
GENTLE CONTEMPLATION
RESTORED PATIENCE

WINTER

SOOTHING SOLITUDE
PEACEFUL REFLECTION
CALM SLOWNESS
REFRESHED WISDOM

WHERE YOU ARE NOW IS NOT WHERE
YOU'LL ALWAYS BE. KEEP GROWING.

OFFLOAD THE BAGGAGE

YOU MIGHT BE CARRYING AROUND MORE EMOTIONAL BAGGAGE
THAN YOU NEED TO, WHICH CERTAINLY DOESN'T HELP WITH
ANXIETY! COLOR IN THESE SUITCASES, AND WRITE SOME THINGS
YOU MIGHT WANT TO OFFLOAD ON THE LUGGAGE TAGS.

PLAY KIND GAMES!

ANXIETY LOVES PLAYING MIND GAMES, BUT LET'S SHIFT THE
FOCUS TO A KIND GAME. ON EACH SQUARE ON THE GAME
BELOW, WRITE SOMETHING KIND YOU CAN DO FOR YOURSELF.
TRY TO DO AT LEAST ONE OF THEM TODAY IF YOU CAN.

THE COLOR ZONE

FEEL LIKE ZONING OUT WITHOUT HAVING TO THINK TOO MUCH?
THIS IS THE PAGE FOR YOU! THE COLOR KEY BELOW TELLS YOU
EXACTLY HOW TO COLOR THIS IN SO YOU CAN ZONE OUT.

1 - PINK/RED 2 - ORANGE 3 - YELLOW
4 - GREEN 5 - BLUE 6 - PURPLE

IT'S ONLY A CHAPTER

IMAGINE YOU'RE LIVING IN A STORYBOOK AS YOU FILL IN THE PAGE BELOW. KEEP IN MIND THAT YOUR CURRENT SITUATION IS ONLY PART OF YOUR STORY, AND WHERE YOU ARE NOW IS ONLY ONE CHAPTER IN THE WHOLE, BIG BOOK OF YOUR LIFE.

SETTING

CHARACTERS

THEMES

CONFLICT

POTENTIAL RESOLUTION

POWERFUL WORDS

TWO OF THE MOST POWERFUL WORDS YOU CAN SAY ARE
"I AM." FILL OUT THE LINES BELOW WITH POSITIVE "I AM"
STATEMENTS, SUCH AS "I AM CAPABLE," "I AM DOING THE BEST I
CAN," OR "I AM MORE THAN HOW I FEEL WHEN I'M ANXIOUS."

I AM _____

I AM _____

I AM _____

I AM _____

I AM _____

I AM _____

I AM _____

I AM _____

I AM _____

I AM _____

I AM _____

I AM _____

MIXED FEELINGS

YOU'RE ALLOWED TO HAVE MIXED FEELINGS ABOUT THE PEOPLE IN YOUR LIFE. CONSIDER SOMEONE YOU HAVE A CHALLENGING RELATIONSHIP WITH AND COLOR IN (WITHOUT JUDGMENT!) THE BOTTLES THAT CORRESPOND WITH HOW YOU FEEL ABOUT THEM.

MAGICAL MUSINGS

IMAGINE YOU VISITED A PSYCHIC AND THEY GAVE YOU THE BEST
POSSIBLE READING FOR YOUR FUTURE. IN THE CRYSTAL BALL,
WRITE WHAT THE PERFECT READING WOULD SAY.

WISH YOU KNEW...

USE THE SPACE BELOW TO WRITE WHAT YOU WISH OTHERS
KNEW ABOUT YOUR ANXIETY. IF YOU FEEL COMFORTABLE, SHARE
THIS WITH A LOVED ONE. IF NOT, KNOW THAT JUST WRITING IT
DOWN CAN BE HELPFUL, EVEN IF YOU NEVER SHARE IT.

i wish you knew...

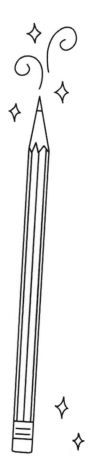

GUIDED GRATITUDE

SOMETIMES IT'S CHALLENGING TO COME UP WITH THINGS TO BE
THANKFUL FOR IN THE MIDST OF ANXIETY, BUT THIS LIST OF
POSITIVE PROMPTS IS HERE TO GUIDE YOUR GRATITUDE.

SOMETHING I LIKE ABOUT MYSELF _____

A SONG I AM GRATEFUL FOR _____

SOMETHING IN NATURE I APPRECIATE _____

A PERSON I FEEL THANKFUL TO KNOW _____

SOMETHING IN THIS ROOM THAT I LOVE _____

A CHARACTERISTIC I'M LUCKY TO HAVE _____

SOMETHING NICE THAT'S HAPPENED TODAY _____

A MEMORY I'LL ALWAYS TREASURE _____

SOMETHING I READ THAT RESONATED _____

A COLOR I REALLY ENJOY SEEING _____

SOMETHING DELICIOUS I LIKE EATING _____

A WORD THAT MAKES ME HAPPY _____

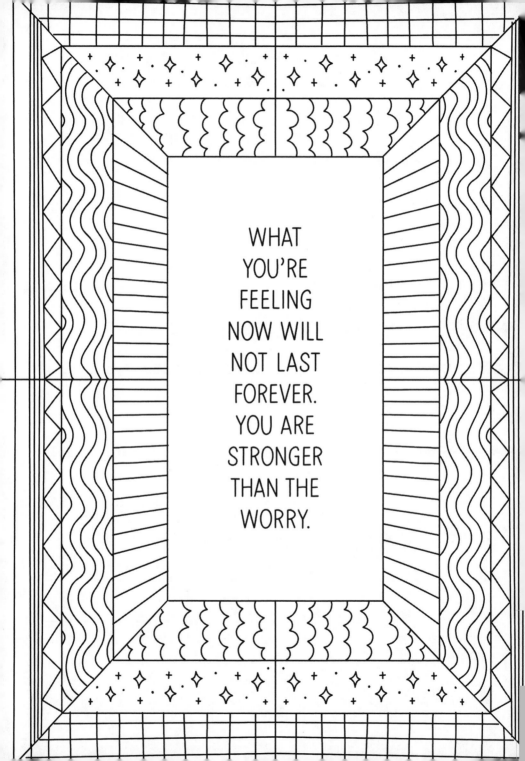

WHAT
YOU'RE
FEELING
NOW WILL
NOT LAST
FOREVER.
YOU ARE
STRONGER
THAN THE
WORRY.

LIGHT UP YOUR LIFE

WHEN YOU'RE FEELING ANXIOUS, WHAT BRIGHTENS YOUR DAY?
BELOW THE LAMPS, WRITE THINGS (BIG OR SMALL!) THAT
BRING YOU JOY. DO YOUR BEST TO SEEK OUT AT LEAST
ONE OF THESE LIFE-BRIGHTENERS TODAY.

CUT IT OUT

WRITE THE FEELINGS, THOUGHTS, OR HABITS YOU'D LIKE TO CUT
OUT OF YOUR LIFE ON THE SCRAPS BELOW. THOUGH YOU
MIGHT NOT BE ABLE TO GET RID OF THEM RIGHT NOW,
KNOWING WHAT YOU DON'T WANT IS HELPFUL!

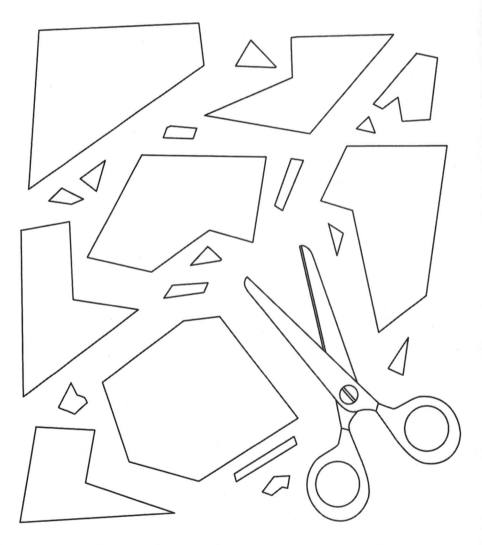

A PEACEFUL PASTIME

HAVING A RELAXING HOBBY CAN HELP WITH ANXIETY. AS
YOU COLOR IN THE PEACEFUL PASTIMES BELOW, CONSIDER
WHETHER ANY OF THEM MIGHT BE WORTH GIVING A TRY.

GARDENING

JOURNALING

SOLITAIRE

EMBROIDERY

PAINTING

HALF EMPTY / HALF FULL

NO MATTER WHAT'S GOING ON, THERE ARE GOOD AND BAD
THINGS HAPPENING. FILL THE BOTTOM HALF OF THE GLASS WITH
NOT-SO-GOOD STUFF AND FILL THE TOP WITH THE GOOD THINGS.
TRY YOUR BEST TO SEE IF YOU CAN PUT MORE UP TOP!

THE
GOOD
STUFF

THE
NOT-SO-GOOD
STUFF

REARVIEW REFLECTION

IN THE REARVIEW MIRROR, WRITE ABOUT ONE THING YOU'VE
OVERCOME IN YOUR LIFE. IT DOESN'T HAVE TO BE A BIG THING,
JUST SOMETHING YOU'RE PROUD TO HAVE ACCOMPLISHED. IF
YOU CAN'T THINK OF ANYTHING, WRITE DOWN WHAT YOU'D
LIKE TO SOMEDAY SEE IN THE REARVIEW MIRROR.

CLOSED EYES, OPEN MIND

PUT YOUR PEN IN THE SQUARE BELOW, CLOSE YOUR EYES, AND
DRAW. EITHER TRY TO DRAW SOMETHING FROM MEMORY OR
SCRIBBLE LIKE WILD. COLOR IN WHATEVER YOU END UP WITH!

SET IT FREE

IF YOU COULD LET GO OF ANY THOUGHTS RIGHT NOW, WHICH ONES WOULD YOU SET FREE? WRITE THEM IN THE BALLOONS WHILE REMINDING YOURSELF THAT YOU WILL EVENTUALLY RELEASE THESE THOUGHTS (EVEN IF YOU'RE NOT READY YET).

PLAYFUL PATTERNS

TAKE TIME OUT FROM YOUR THOUGHTS TO COLOR IN THE
PATTERNS. LISTEN TO SOME UPLIFTING MUSIC IF YOU CAN!

ANXIETY INVESTIGATION

A LOT OF ASPECTS GO INTO THE CREATION OF ANXIOUS
EMOTIONS. ON THE BOARD BELOW, FILL OUT WHAT MIGHT BE
OCCURRING IN THOSE CATEGORIES TO ADD TO YOUR ANXIETY.

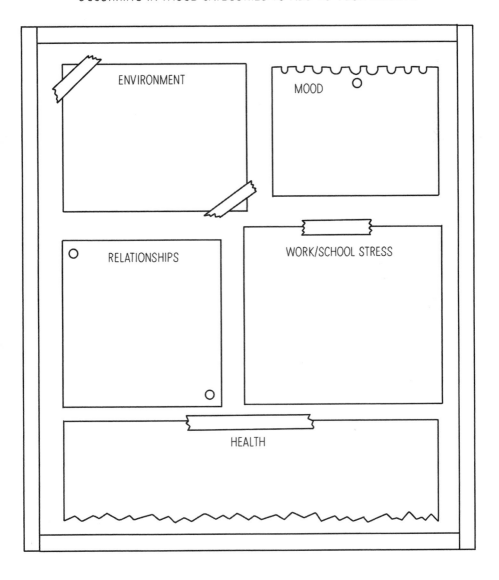

ENVIRONMENT

MOOD

RELATIONSHIPS

WORK/SCHOOL STRESS

HEALTH

YOU ALREADY KNOW
THIS, BUT HERE'S A
REMINDER ANYWAY:
EVERYTHING IS
TEMPORARY.

CLEVER CROSSWORD

PAUSE YOUR WORRIES FOR A BIT AND FILL OUT THE
CROSSWORD PUZZLE BELOW. IT'LL GIVE YOU A LITTLE BREAK!

ACROSS

2. KNOWLEDGE ABOUT YOURSELF
4. WHAT YOU MIGHT SEEK WHEN STRESSED
5. QUALITY OF BEING THANKFUL
6. A FEELING OF RELAXATION
11. EXPECTATION OF GOOD THINGS HAPPENING
12. A SYNONYM FOR "EMOTIONS"

DOWN

1. ONE OF THE BEST MEDICINES
3. A BODILY FUNCTION THAT CAN CREATE CALM
7. AN EMOTION YOU MAY BE FEELING
8. SEEK THIS WHEN YOU WANT TO BE UPLIFTED
9. THE OPPOSITE OF NEGATIVITY
10. A SLOGAN FOR STAYING IN THE MOMENT

ANSWER KEY AT THE END OF THE BOOK!

FILL YOUR VASE

FLOWERS NEED WATER TO THRIVE. FOR YOU TO THRIVE, SELF-COMPASSION IS NEEDED. FILL THE VASE WITH ENCOURAGING WORDS YOU'D LIKE TO HEAR. IF YOU'RE NOT SURE WHAT TO WRITE, IMAGINE WHAT YOU'D TELL AN ANXIOUS FRIEND.

RANK YOUR MOOD

INVESTIGATE YOUR EMOTIONAL STATE BY COLORING IN THE
BLOCKS BELOW. 1 MEANS YOU'RE BARELY FEELING IT, WHILE 10
MEANS IT'S A DOMINATING EMOTION RIGHT NOW.

RELAXED

1	2	3	4	5	6	7	8	9	10

STRESSED

1	2	3	4	5	6	7	8	9	10

OPTIMISTIC

1	2	3	4	5	6	7	8	9	10

CONFUSED

1	2	3	4	5	6	7	8	9	10

INSPIRED

1	2	3	4	5	6	7	8	9	10

DISTRESSED

1	2	3	4	5	6	7	8	9	10

JOYFUL

1	2	3	4	5	6	7	8	9	10

BUILD YOUR BOUNDARIES

SETTING BOUNDARIES IS ESSENTIAL FOR COPING WITH ANXIETY.
IT CAN BE CHALLENGING TO SET BOUNDARIES, BUT THE FIRST
STEP IS KNOWING WHAT BOUNDARIES MIGHT BE HELPFUL.

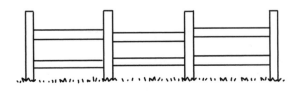

A BOUNDARY I'D LIKE TO SET WITH A FAMILY MEMBER

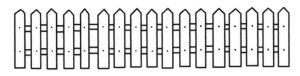

A BOUNDARY I'D LIKE TO SET WITH PEOPLE AT WORK/SCHOOL

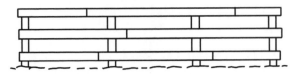

A BOUNDARY I'D LIKE TO SET WITH A FRIEND

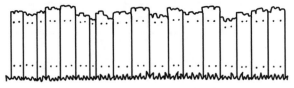

A BOUNDARY I'D LIKE TO SET WITH PEOPLE I DON'T KNOW WELL

ANXIETY ATTACK PLAN

WHEN YOU'RE IN A GOOD EMOTIONAL STATE, FILL OUT THE
WORKSHEET BELOW. BOOKMARK THIS PAGE AND COME BACK TO
IT WHEN YOU'RE HAVING AN INCREDIBLY ANXIOUS DAY.

THINGS THAT OFTEN
INCREASE MY ANXIETY
AND SHOULD BE
AVOIDED RIGHT NOW

FOUR POSITIVE DISTRACTIONS I CAN TRY

CRISIS HOTLINE OR
THERAPIST'S NUMBER

CALMING PEOPLE I CAN CALL OR TEXT

COPING TACTICS THAT HAVE HELPED IN THE PAST

PUZZLE PAUSE

WHEN YOU FEEL PUZZLED BY LIFE, TAKE A BREAK AND FOCUS
ON COLORING IN THE PUZZLE BELOW, REMINDING YOURSELF
THAT YOU DON'T HAVE TO FIGURE EVERYTHING OUT RIGHT NOW.

THOUGHT WEATHER

THOUGHTS ARE LIKE THE WEATHER—THEY COME AND THEY GO.
ON THE CLOUDS BELOW, WRITE DOWN THE THOUGHTS
DOMINATING YOUR MIND RIGHT NOW. REMEMBER: NO MATTER
HOW STRONG THEY MIGHT FEEL, THEY WON'T LAST FOREVER.

MAGIC WORDS

THE WORDS WE USE HAVE A MAGICAL IMPACT ON HOW WE SEE
THE WORLD. IN THE SPEECH BUBBLES BELOW, WRITE EVERY
POSITIVE ADJECTIVE YOU CAN THINK OF TO DESCRIBE YOUR LIFE,
AND COME BACK TO THIS PAGE WHEN YOU'RE FEELING LOW.

EMOTIONAL EASEL

ON THE EASEL, DRAW HOW YOU'RE FEELING RIGHT NOW.
IF CREATING ART ISN'T YOUR THING, JUST SCRIBBLE OR
DOODLE OR WRITE OUT YOUR FEELINGS.

YOU ARE
STRONGER,
BIGGER,
BRAVER,
AND BETTER
THAN WHAT'S
WORRYING YOU
RIGHT NOW.

LEAVE YOUR WORRIES

HERE'S A TRICK FOR LEAVING YOUR OWN WORRIES BEHIND:
HELP SOMEONE ELSE! AS YOU COLOR IN THE IDEAS FOR HELPING
OTHERS, CONSIDER WHICH ONES YOU'D LIKE TO TRY SOON
(OR EVEN TODAY!).

WORD NERD

LOOK AROUND YOUR ROOM. ON THE LEFT, WRITE DOWN AS MANY
THINGS AS YOU CAN SEE. ON THE RIGHT, SEE HOW MANY WORDS
YOU CAN MAKE FROM THE LETTERS IN THE WORDS YOU WROTE.

WORDS	WORDS FROM WORDS
LAMP	AMP, LAP, LAM, MAP, AM, PALM, PAL

CIRCLE OF GRATITUDE

GRATITUDE IS AN ESSENTIAL ANXIETY-FIGHTING SKILL! SHARPEN
YOUR GRATITUDE BY FILLING IN EACH SECTION OF THE PIE CHART
WITH SOMETHING YOU'RE THANKFUL TO HAVE IN YOUR LIFE.

INSPIRING I-SPY

CHOOSE A COLOR FOR EACH OF THE SHAPES BELOW AND COLOR
THEM IN, ONE SHAPE AT A TIME. THIS WILL ENCOURAGE YOU TO
FOCUS ON THE PRESENT, STEPPING AWAY FROM ANXIETY.

♡ 7   ☆ 5   ☾ 5   ◯ 12   ♦ 5   ✳ 9   ✦ 12

☁ 6   ◇ 16   ◎ 5   ⬭ 7   ▽ 22   ♡ 17

CEREBRAL CHECK-IN

IF YOU'RE FEELING UP TO IT, FILL OUT THE BOXES WITH
HOW YOU'RE CURRENTLY FEELING. PERIODICALLY COME BACK
TO THIS PAGE AND CHECK IN WITH THESE PROMPTS.

A MOMENT I FELT STRONG TODAY...	SOMETHING THAT FEELS HARD NOW...	A LESSON I'M GLAD TO HAVE LEARNED...
RIGHT NOW I AM GRATEFUL FOR...	I WANT TO FORGIVE MYSELF FOR...	I CAN'T STOP THINKING ABOUT...
A CHANGE I'D LIKE TO MAKE...	I WOULD LIKE TO LET GO OF...	WHAT IS INSPIRING ME TO KEEP GOING...

DISTRACTION IN ACTION

DISTRACTION CAN BE A GREAT TOOL TO GET OUT OF AN ANXIOUS
THOUGHT SPIRAL. DISTRACT YOURSELF WITH THESE (RANDOM!)
QUESTIONS AND SEE WHAT YOU LEARN ABOUT YOURSELF.

WHAT IS THE MOST INTERESTING
ITEM IN YOUR HOME?

WHAT IS YOUR FAVORITE MOVIE OR BOOK?

IF THIS WEEK WERE A SONG,
WHAT WOULD THE TITLE BE?

WHAT WAS THE LAST THING THAT
MADE YOU LAUGH REALLY HARD?

WHAT'S SOMETHING ABOUT YOU THAT WOULD
PROBABLY SURPRISE OTHER PEOPLE?

ARE THERE ANY WORDS
YOU LOVE OR HATE?

WHEN WAS THE LAST TIME YOU DID
SOMETHING FOR THE FIRST TIME?

"I WANT TO FEEL..."

COLOR IN THE ITEM (OR ITEMS!) THAT BEST REPRESENTS HOW YOU'D LIKE TO FEEL. WHAT COULD YOU DO TODAY (OR SOON, IF TODAY ISN'T AN OPTION) TO GET CLOSER TO THAT FEELING?

A SLOWLY FLOWING HOURGLASS, BALANCING THE PASSAGE OF TIME

A VIBRANT ROSE GARDEN NEWLY IN FULL BLOOM

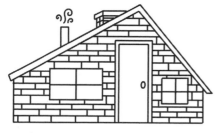

A COZY CABIN LIT WARMLY FROM WITHIN BY A CRACKLING FIRE

A BELOVED OLD SWEATER, WORN-IN AT ALL THE RIGHT PLACES

A SPARKLING MIRRORBALL, LIGHTING UP THE DANCE FLOOR

(SELF) LOVE LETTER

ON THE LETTER BELOW, WRITE A LOVE LETTER TO YOUR PAST SELF, CELEBRATING HOW FAR YOU'VE COME, WHAT YOU'VE OVERCOME, AND ALL THE TIMES YOU'VE KEPT GOING.

GUILT-FREE QUILT

AS YOU COLOR IN THE QUILT BELOW, REMIND YOURSELF THAT
YOU SHOULDN'T FEEL GUILTY FOR TAKING TIME FOR YOURSELF
WHEN YOU'RE ANXIOUS. YOU ARE WORTHY OF SELF-CARE.

TODAY MAY NOT BE
A GREAT DAY, BUT TOMORROW
IS A FRESH START.
DON'T GIVE UP ON YOURSELF.

POSITIVE POPSICLES

REVIEW THE OPTIONS BELOW AND COLOR IN THE POSITIVE
POPSICLE(S) YOU MOST NEED IN YOUR LIFE RIGHT NOW.

PEACE OF MIND   TRUE CONNECTION   GOOD NEWS   SOFT COMFORT

NEW PERSPECTIVE   ZERO DOUBTS   SAFE FREEDOM   ACCEPTANCE OF NOW

DUMP YOUR BRAIN

IN THE THOUGHT BUBBLE BELOW, WRITE EVERY THOUGHT THAT
COMES TO MIND. IT CAN BE SURPRISINGLY HELPFUL TO GET
THOUGHTS OUT OF YOUR HEAD AND ONTO THE PAGE!

MINDFUL MAZE

MAKE YOUR WAY THROUGH THE MAZE BELOW, COLLECTING AND
COLORING THE ICONS OF SELF-COMPASSION ALONG THE WAY!

START

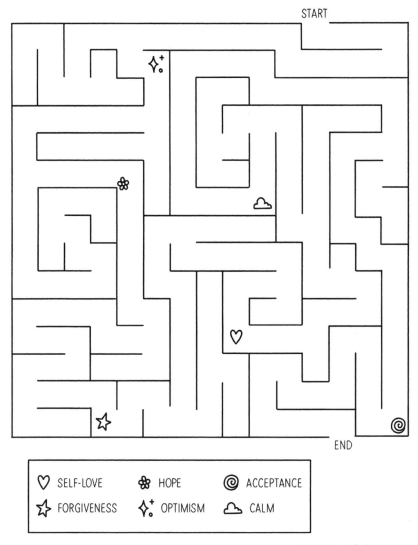

END

♡ SELF-LOVE	✿ HOPE	◎ ACCEPTANCE
☆ FORGIVENESS	✦ OPTIMISM	☁ CALM

ANSWER KEY AT THE END OF THE BOOK!

LIFE IS (SOMETIMES) SWEET

WHEN ANXIETY STRIKES, IT'S TOUGH TO REMEMBER LIFE'S
SWEETNESS, BUT IT'S STILL THERE, UNDERNEATH IT ALL. WRITE
SOME OF LIFE'S SWEETEST THINGS ON THE CANDY BELOW.

BOTHERSOME BUTTONS

IF YOU'RE HAVING A DECENT DAY,* WRITE SOME ANXIETY
TRIGGERS ON THE BUTTONS BELOW SO YOU'LL HAVE A
REMINDER OF THINGS TO AVOID IN THE FUTURE.

* IF YOU'RE ALREADY SUPER STRESSED, THIS PROBABLY
ISN'T THE BEST PAGE. FLIP TO ANOTHER ONE TODAY!

MIRROR MINDED

LIFE IS A REFLECTION OF HOW YOU VIEW THE WORLD.
ON THE MIRROR BELOW, WRITE WHAT AN IDEAL LIFE (OR DAY,
IF LIFE IS TOO BIG TO TACKLE) WOULD LOOK LIKE.

TAKE YOUR PICK

SHADE IN THE BITS OF PAPER YOU'D MOST LIKE TO BE
REMINDED OF RIGHT NOW. THEN ASK SOMEONE YOU TRUST IF
THEY MIGHT BE ABLE TO HELP YOU CULTIVATE THOSE IDEAS.

take the
REMINDER
you NEED

TRUST YOURSELF.

THE PAST DOESN'T
EQUAL THE FUTURE.

THIS WILL PASS.

MISTAKES ARE OKAY.

IT'S NOT TOO LATE
TO BEGIN AGAIN.

YOU DESERVE LOVE
AND RELAXATION.

THERE ARE STILL
BEAUTIFUL THINGS.

BUBBLE BUDDIES

FILL EACH SEGMENT OF THE OVERLAPPING BUBBLES BELOW
WITH A DIFFERENT COLOR OR PATTERN. AS YOU DO THIS, FOCUS
ON THE IDEA THAT EVERYTHING IS CONNECTED AND YOU ARE
NOT ALONE (EVEN WHEN YOU FEEL LIKE YOU ARE).

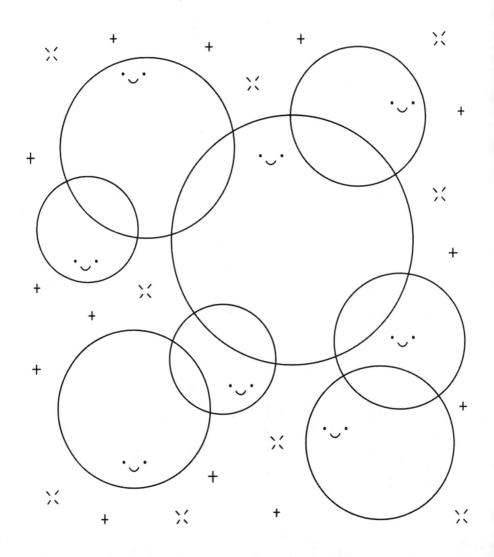

HOME SWEET HOME

IN EACH OF THE ROOMS, WRITE OR DRAW WHAT YOU NEED TO
FEEL COMFORTABLE AT HOME, PAYING SPECIAL ATTENTION TO
WHAT YOU ALREADY POSSESS IN YOUR HOME NOW.

TRY NOT TO
LABEL YOUR FEELINGS
AS "GOOD" OR "BAD."
ALL OF YOUR EMOTIONS
HAVE A PURPOSE.

DEAR FUTURE SELF

WRITE LETTERS TO YOUR FUTURE SELVES ON THE POSTCARDS
BELOW, SHARING HOW YOU'RE FEELING NOW AND/OR HOW YOU
HOPE TO BE FEELING AS THAT FUTURE VERSION OF YOU.

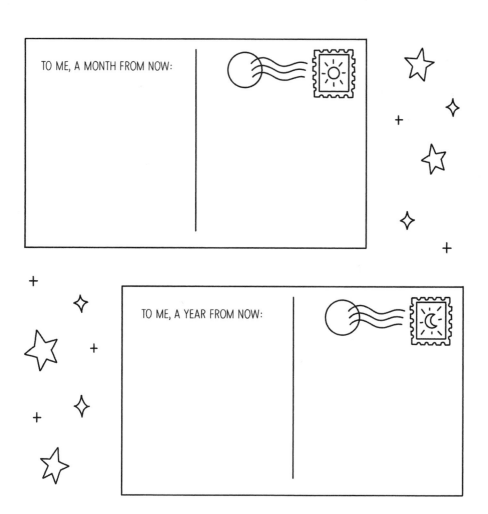

TO ME, A MONTH FROM NOW:

TO ME, A YEAR FROM NOW:

REFRESHING REPHRASING

THE MIND OFTEN DISREGARDS THE WORD "NOT." TRY
EXPERIMENTING WITH AVOIDING USING NEGATIVE WORDS TO
DESCRIBE YOUR EMOTIONS. INSTEAD, TRY USING "NOT"
IN FRONT OF A FEELING YOU WANT TO FEEL.

ORIGINAL THOUGHT	THOUGHT WITH DESIRED FEELING INCLUDED
"I AM ANXIOUS."	"I AM NOT CALM."

SERENE STATEMENTS

READ THROUGH THE PHRASES BELOW AND CHOOSE THE THREE
YOU MOST NEED TO HEAR. COLOR IN THE ILLUSTRATIONS ON
THOSE WHILE REPEATING THE PHRASES TO YOURSELF.

LET'S GET PHYSICAL

TAKE A MENTAL SCAN OF YOUR BODY, AND FILL IN ANY AREAS
THAT ARE FEELING TIGHT, HEAVY, UNEASY, OR TENSE WITH THE
CORRESPONDING PATTERNS SHOWN BELOW.

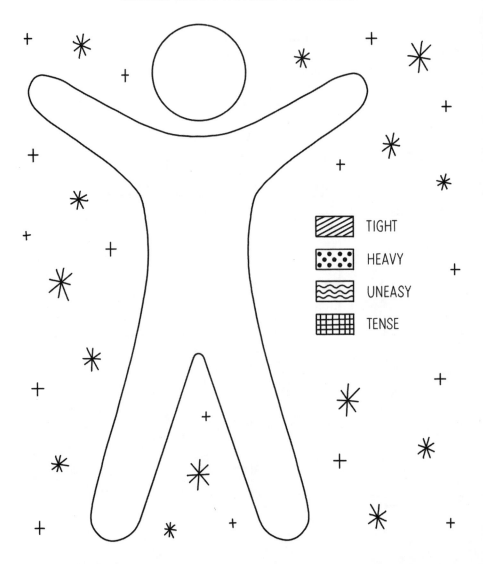

A HIVE OF WORDS

ANYONE WITH ANXIETY CAN LIKELY RELATE TO VIRGINIA WOOLF'S WORDS: "MY HEAD IS A HIVE OF WORDS THAT WON'T SETTLE." ON THE HIVE BELOW, WRITE DOWN ANY THOUGHTS THAT ARE CIRCLING AROUND IN YOUR HEAD RIGHT NOW.

FEEL THE FUTURE

AS YOU COLOR IN THE CARDS BELOW, REFLECT ON WHAT IT WILL
FEEL LIKE TO BE CALM, JOYFUL, AND AT EASE. THOSE FEELINGS
MIGHT SEEM FAR FROM REACH NOW, BUT THE FUTURE IS
SURPRISING AND YOU VERY WELL MIGHT FEEL THEM SOON.

STILL LEARNING

LEARNING SHOULDN'T END AT THE CLASSROOM DOOR. ON THE
CHALKBOARD, WRITE EITHER: (1) THINGS YOU'VE LEARNED
OUTSIDE OF SCHOOL, OR (2) THINGS YOU'D LIKE TO LEARN.

BLOOMING BREATHING

WHEN YOU'RE EXTRA STRESSED, USE THIS PAGE AS A POINT OF PAUSE. FOLLOW THE INSTRUCTIONS ON THE FLOWER PETALS, REPEATING AS NEEDED. (NOTE: SOMETIMES BREATHING EXERCISES INCREASE ANXIETY, SO STOP IF IT FEELS OFF.)

START HERE

WORRIED WARNINGS

YOUR BODY OFTEN SENDS SIGNALS WHEN YOU'RE WORRIED. ON
THE SIGNS BELOW, WRITE SOME OF THE WARNING SIGNS YOU
GET FROM YOUR BODY (HEART RACING, SWEATING, ETC.).

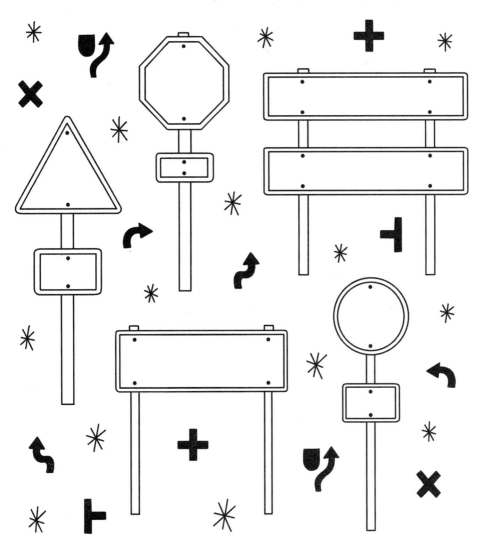

YOU ARE MORE
VALUABLE THAN
WHAT YOU DID TODAY.
PRODUCTIVITY ISN'T
A MEASURE OF
A GOOD DAY.

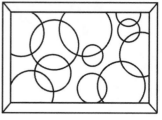

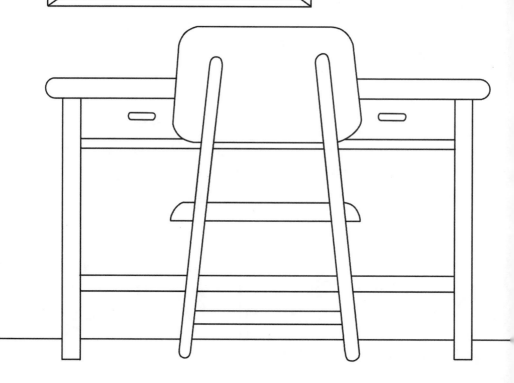

SELF EXPLORATION

IDENTIFYING (OR DISCOVERING!) FACTS ABOUT YOURSELF CAN BE
FUN—OR AT LEAST A MUCH-NEEDED DISTRACTION FROM
ANXIETY! SEE WHAT YOU FIND IN YOUR ANSWERS BELOW.

I AM SOMEONE WHO LOVES TO _____

I AM SOMEONE WHO WOULD NEVER _____

I AM SOMEONE WHO ALWAYS _____

I AM SOMEONE WHO ISN'T A FAN OF _____

I AM SOMEONE WHO WILL SOMEDAY _____

I AM SOMEONE WHO IS INSPIRED BY _____

I AM SOMEONE WHO STRUGGLES WITH _____

I AM SOMEONE WHO WANTS TO _____

I AM SOMEONE WHO WISHES THEY COULD _____

I AM SOMEONE WHO IS GOOD AT _____

I AM SOMEONE WHO USED TO _____

I AM SOMEONE WHO OFTEN FEELS _____

I AM SOMEONE WHO CAN _____

SCRIBBLE IT OUT

ASSIGN A COLOR TO EACH OF THE EMOTIONS IN THE KEY BELOW.
THEN TAKE EACH COLOR AND SCRIBBLE INSIDE THE CIRCLE AS
MUCH YOU WANT TO LET OUT SOME OF THOSE EMOTIONS!

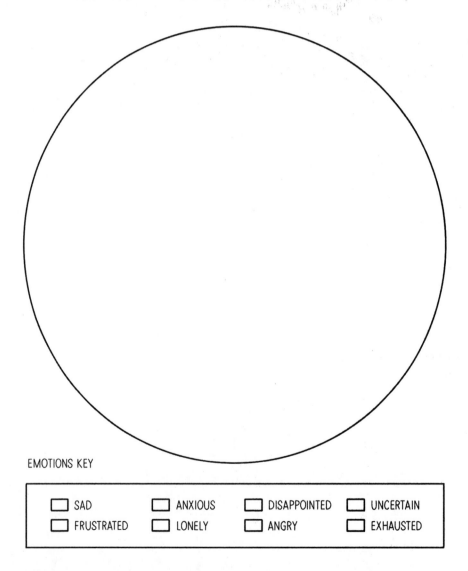

EMOTIONS KEY

☐ SAD   ☐ ANXIOUS   ☐ DISAPPOINTED   ☐ UNCERTAIN
☐ FRUSTRATED   ☐ LONELY   ☐ ANGRY   ☐ EXHAUSTED

SPOT THE DIFFERENCES

LOOK FOR 20 DIFFERENCES BETWEEN THE TWO GARDENS.
SEARCHING FOR THESE IRREGULARITIES WILL GIVE YOUR MIND A
FOCUSED CHALLENGE TO DISTRACT FROM ANXIOUS THINKING.

ANSWER KEY AT THE END OF THE BOOK!

TINTED THOUGHTS

CHOOSE A COLOR FOR EACH HEART, AND AS YOU'RE COLORING THEM IN, CONSIDER HOW YOUR THOUGHTS MIGHT HAVE BEEN TINTED BY WHAT YOU'VE SEEN, FELT, OR EXPERIENCED TODAY.

YOUR THOUGHTS ARE
INFLUENCED BY WHAT YOU...

LOVE

SEE

DO

READ

BELIEVE

HEAR

FEEL

WANT

TODAY HAVE YOU...

IT'S NORMAL FOR TO-DO LISTS TO BE ABANDONED IN ANXIOUS TIMES, BUT TAKE A LOOK AT THE LIST BELOW AND SEE IF YOU HAVE DONE (OR CAN DO) ANY OF THESE THINGS TODAY. IF NOT, DON'T WORRY! JUST COLOR IN THIS PAGE AND KEEP BREATHING.

- GOTTEN OUT OF BED
- TAKEN YOUR MEDS (IF NEEDED)
- DONE SOMETHING CREATIVE
- READ A BOOK OR ANY NON-NEWS CONTENT
- EATEN AT LEAST ONE MEAL OR SNACK
- BEEN GRATEFUL FOR SOMETHING
- TAKEN A SHOWER OR BATH
- LISTENED TO MUSIC THAT FEELS GOOD
- STRETCHED OR MOVED YOUR BODY
- WRITTEN ABOUT YOUR FEELINGS
- TALKED TO OR TEXTED A FRIEND
- PRACTICED SELF-COMPASSION
- SPENT (EVEN A LITTLE) TIME OUTSIDE
- LAUGHED AT SOMETHING FUNNY
- ASKED FOR HELP IF YOU NEEDED IT
- REMINDED YOURSELF THAT YOU'RE OKAY
- TAKEN BREAKS WHEN OVERWHELMED
- DONE SOMETHING THAT COMFORTS YOU
- ACKNOWLEDGED YOUR SMALL WINS

MEMORY LANE

DURING A STRESSFUL TIME, IT CAN BE HELPFUL TO REMIND
YOURSELF IT HASN'T ALWAYS BEEN (AND WON'T ALWAYS BE!)
THIS WAY. ON THE BUILDINGS BELOW, WRITE DOWN FOUR OF
YOUR HAPPIEST MEMORIES AND KNOW YOU'LL HAVE MORE.

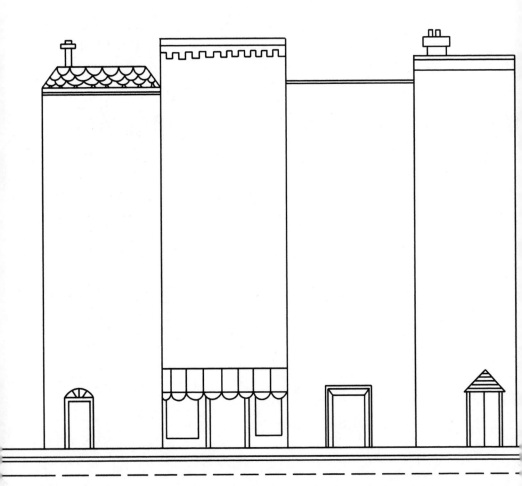

WHICH SUN ARE YOU?

EACH SUN BELOW HAS BEEN PAIRED WITH A DIFFERENT
EMOTIONAL STATE. COLOR IN THE ONES THAT ARE THE
MOST RELATABLE TO YOU TODAY.

FRUSTRATED WITH THE
CURRENT SITUATION

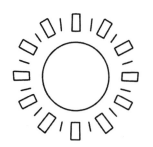

EXCITED AND READY
TO EMBRACE THE DAY

RELAXED AND AT
EASE WITH EVERYTHING

INSPIRED BY LOTS
OF NEW IDEAS

WORRIED ABOUT
WHAT'S COMING NEXT

OVERWHELMED BY
A LONG TO-DO LIST

IMPORTANT REMINDER!

WE GET SO ATTACHED TO OUR THOUGHTS THAT WE OFTEN
FORGET WE ARE MORE THAN WHAT WE THINK. AS YOU COLOR
IN THE LETTERS, REPEAT THIS PHRASE TO YOURSELF.

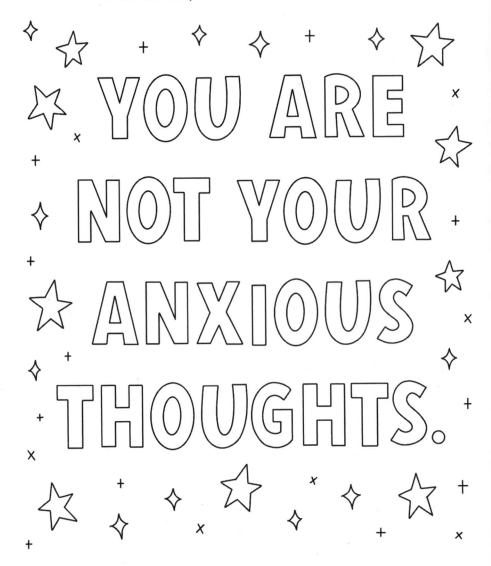

YOU ARE NOT YOUR ANXIOUS THOUGHTS.

CELEBRATE YOURSELF

YOU'VE COME A LONG WAY, AND YOU SHOULD BE PROUD OF YOURSELF! IN THE SPACE BELOW, WRITE A LIST OF ALL THE THINGS YOU'VE DONE OR OVERCOME. (THEY CAN BE BIG OR AS SMALL AS "GOT OUT OF BED ON A HARD DAY.")

LOOKING FOR THE GOOD WON'T REMOVE ANXIETY, BUT IT MIGHT CHANGE HOW IT FEELS. OPT FOR OPTIMISM.

MEET YOUR ANXIETY

ON A DAY WHEN YOU'RE FEELING PRETTY GOOD, FILL OUT THIS WORKSHEET. THESE QUESTIONS WILL HELP YOU UNDERSTAND YOUR ANXIETY AND CAN BE A REFERENCE TO RETURN TO LATER.

WHAT PHYSICAL SYMPTOMS DO YOU EXPERIENCE WHEN YOU'RE ANXIOUS? CIRCLE ANY THAT APPLY AND/OR ADD YOUR OWN ON THE BLANK LINES.

SWEATING	TROUBLE BREATHING	OVER/UNDERSLEEPING	_____
FAST HEARTBEAT	HEADACHE	LACK OF FOCUS	_____
SHAKING/CHILLS	RESTLESSNESS	NUMBNESS/TINGLING	_____
IRRITABILITY	OVER/UNDEREATING	FATIGUE	_____
STOMACHACHE	DIZZINESS	MUSCLE TENSION	_____

WHAT ARE SOME THINGS, PEOPLE, OR EXPERIENCES THAT ARE LIKELY TO TRIGGER YOUR ANXIETY? (BE AS HONEST AS POSSIBLE—JUST BECAUSE SOMETHING TRIGGERS ANXIETY, THAT DOESN'T MEAN IT'S "BAD.")

_____

_____

_____

_____

WHAT ARE SOME TACTICS, THOUGHTS, PEOPLE, OR THINGS THAT HAVE HELPED ALLEVIATE YOUR ANXIETY IN THE PAST?

_____

_____

_____

_____

WHAT DO YOU WISH FRIENDS, FAMILY, AND LOVED ONES KNEW ABOUT YOUR ANXIETY? WHAT MIGHT THEY BE ABLE TO DO TO HELP YOU COPE WITH IT?

_____

_____

_____

_____

YOU ARE AN ARTIST

LET'S USE YOUR CREATIVE SKILLS TO COLOR IN THE FAMOUS
ARTWORKS BELOW. YOU CAN LOOK UP THE ORIGINALS
FOR INSPIRATION OR JUST WING IT!

BIJUTSU SEKAI (1893-1896)

JULIE DE GRAAG (1877-1924)

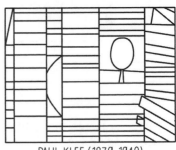

PAUL KLEE (1879-1940)

HANNAH BORGER OVERBECK (1870-1931)

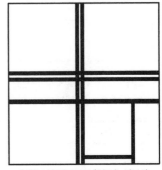

PIET MONDRIAN (1872-1944)

LET-IT-GO LEAVES

CLINGING TO WHAT'S NO LONGER SERVING YOU CAN INCREASE
ANXIETY. ON THE LINES BELOW, WRITE DOWN WHAT YOU'D LIKE
TO RELEASE (BUT NO PRESSURE TO LET GO JUST YET!).

RETURN TO GRATITUDE

CHALLENGING ANXIETY WITH GRATITUDE IS OFTEN A GREAT
WAY TO DISRUPT UNHELPFUL RUMINATION. IF YOU'RE STUCK IN
YOUR THOUGHTS, USE THIS PAGE TO RETURN TO GRATITUDE.

SOMETHING INSPIRING

_____

A SKILL I POSSESS

_____

A LAUGH-OUT-LOUD MEMORY

_____

A PART OF NATURE

_____

SOMETHING COMFORTING

_____

A RELATIONSHIP (PAST OR PRESENT)

_____

SOMETHING INTANGIBLE

_____

A ONCE-IN-A-LIFETIME MOMENT

_____

AN EMOTION

_____

DOES IT HELP OR HURT?

CONSIDER THE ACTIVITIES YOU'VE DONE TODAY. ON THE LEFT, WRITE THE ONES THAT HELPED YOU FEEL LESS ANXIOUS. ON THE RIGHT, WRITE THE ONES THAT WERE HURTFUL (OR LESS HELPFUL). USE THIS AS A GUIDE FOR TOMORROW.

HELPFUL ACTIVITIES

HURTFUL ACTIVITIES

GARDEN OF GROWTH

ANXIETY IS IN NO WAY REQUIRED FOR GROWTH. BUT GROWTH IS
POSSIBLE IN SPITE OF—AND SOMETIMES BECAUSE OF—
ANXIETY. ON THE SIGNS BELOW, WRITE THREE WAYS ANXIETY
MIGHT HAVE HELPED YOU GROW (OR HOW YOU'D LIKE IT TO).

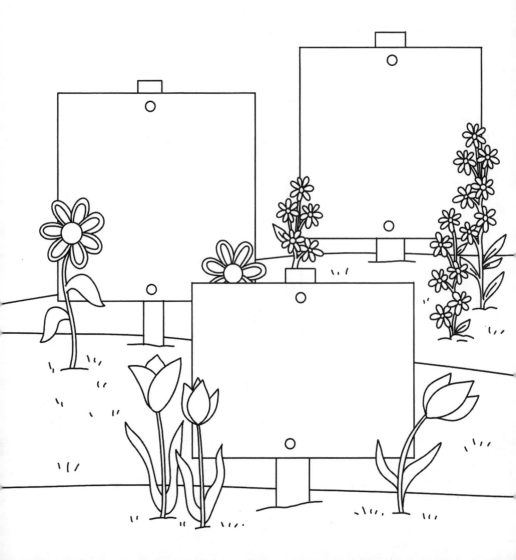

CHANGE THE CHANNEL

YOUR MIND IS LIKE A TV AND YOUR THOUGHTS ARE THE
CHANNELS. AS YOU COLOR IN THE DRAWING BELOW, CONSIDER
WHAT CHANNEL YOU'D LIKE YOUR MIND TO BE ON.

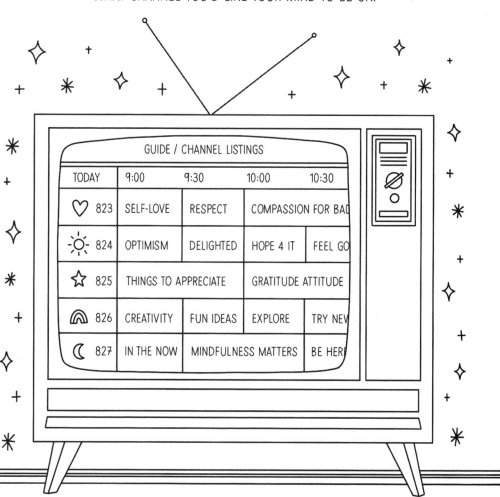

GUIDE / CHANNEL LISTINGS

TODAY	9:00	9:30	10:00	10:30
♡ 823	SELF-LOVE	RESPECT	COMPASSION FOR BA[	
☀ 824	OPTIMISM	DELIGHTED	HOPE 4 IT	FEEL GO
☆ 825	THINGS TO APPRECIATE		GRATITUDE ATTITUDE	
⌒ 826	CREATIVITY	FUN IDEAS	EXPLORE	TRY NEW
☾ 827	IN THE NOW	MINDFULNESS MATTERS		BE HER[

CATCH YOUR THOUGHTS

FILL OUT THE QUESTIONS BELOW TO PRACTICE CATCHING YOUR
ANXIOUS THOUGHTS BEFORE THEY OVERWHELM YOU. THIS
TAKES PRACTICE, SO IT'S OKAY IF THIS IS CHALLENGING.

WHAT SITUATION IS MAKING YOU FEEL ANXIOUS RIGHT NOW?

WHAT IS THE BEST POSSIBLE OUTCOME?

WHAT IS THE WORST POSSIBLE OUTCOME?

WHAT IS THE MOST LIKELY OUTCOME?

REGARDLESS OF THE OUTCOME, HOW WILL YOU FEEL ABOUT THIS SITUATION A WEEK FROM NOW?
IN A YEAR? IN FIVE YEARS?

IS THERE ANY ACTION YOU CAN TAKE (RELATED TO THE SITUATION OR TO YOUR MENTAL STATE) TO
EASE YOUR ANXIETY ABOUT THIS RIGHT NOW?

TIE ONE ON

IF YOU COULD GIVE YOURSELF ONE OF THE FRIENDSHIP
BRACELETS BELOW, WHICH ONE WOULD YOU CHOOSE?
COLOR THAT ONE IN AS YOU BRAINSTORM WAYS YOU
CAN BRING THAT FEELING INTO YOUR LIFE TODAY.

IT'S OKAY IF YOU NEED A LOT OF
ALONE TIME TO STAY SHARP.

UNDER YOUR UMBRELLA

ON THE PANELS OF THE UMBRELLA BELOW, WRITE FOUR THINGS
YOU CAN DO TO COMFORT YOURSELF WHEN YOU'RE FEELING
ANXIOUS. (TRY TO THINK OF THINGS YOU CAN DO ANYWHERE
WITHOUT ANY SPECIAL TOOLS OR INPUT FROM OTHERS.)

WORD OF THE WEEK

WRITE EACH WORD THREE TIMES (IN DIFFERENT COLORS IF YOU LIKE!). THEN CHOOSE YOUR FAVORITE AS YOUR "WORD OF THE WEEK." TRY TO INCORPORATE IT INTO EACH DAY FOR A WEEK.

PEACE   _____   _____   _____

OPTIMISM   _____   _____   _____

JOY   _____   _____   _____

ENERGY   _____   _____   _____

GRATITUDE   _____   _____   _____

FOCUS   _____   _____   _____

CALM   _____   _____   _____

GROWTH   _____   _____   _____

LOVE   _____   _____   _____

PURPOSE   _____   _____   _____

HOPE   _____   _____   _____

COURAGE   _____   _____   _____

STRENGTH   _____   _____   _____

WORD OF THE WEEK:

GO WITH THE FLOW

CHOOSE ONE THING YOU'RE FEELING RIGHT NOW, AND WRITE
ABOUT HOW IT FEELS IN YOUR MIND, IN YOUR HEART, AND
IN YOUR BODY. PAY ATTENTION TO THE WAY IT FEELS TO
ACCEPT THE EMOTION AND GO WITH ITS FLOW.

ANXIETY INQUIRY

IF YOU'RE UP FOR DOING SOME SOUL-SEARCHING, GIVE SOME
THOUGHT TO THE QUESTIONS BELOW. IF THEY FEEL HEAVY, FEEL
FREE TO COME BACK TO THIS PAGE AT A LATER DATE.

WHAT DO I WANT RIGHT NOW?

WHAT DO I FEEL ATTACHED TO?

WHAT AM I AFRAID WILL HAPPEN?

WHAT IS BEST FOR ME NOW?

WHY IS IT CHALLENGING TO ACCEPT?

WHAT LESSONS CAN I LEARN FROM THIS?

WHAT WOULD EMPOWER ME NOW?

FEAR FIGHTERS

BELOW YOU'LL FIND SOME SUGGESTIONS FOR FIGHTING FEAR.
CIRCLE THE ONES THAT FEEL MOST ATTAINABLE TO YOU RIGHT
NOW, AND COLOR IN THE PAGE AS YOU REFLECT ON THEM.

WHEN IT WORKED OUT

ON THE PAGE BELOW, WRITE ABOUT A TIME YOU FELT ANXIOUS
BUT THE SITUATION WORKED OUT BETTER THAN EXPECTED OR
DIDN'T HAPPEN AT ALL. (THIS OCCURS OFTEN, SO KEEP THIS IN
MIND THE NEXT TIME YOU'RE FILLED WITH ANXIETY!)

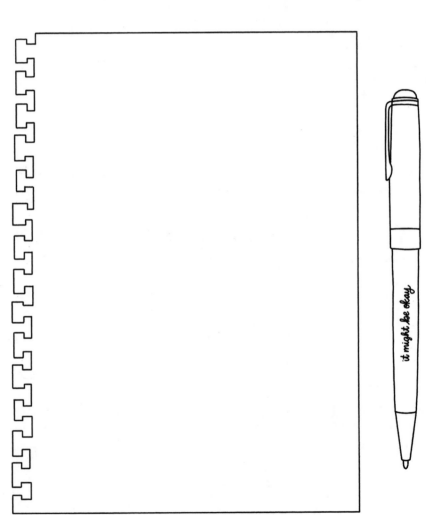

it might be okay

SUNNY THOUGHTS

ON THE SHAPES SURROUNDING THE SUN, WRITE DOWN THINGS
THAT BRING YOU JOY, LIKE "THE WAG OF A DOG'S TAIL," "THE
SMILE OF SOMEONE I LOVE," OR "HEARING MY FAVORITE SONG."
COME BACK TO THIS PAGE WHEN YOU NEED A PICK-ME-UP!

STELLAR BREATHING

PAYING ATTENTION TO YOUR BREATHING CAN HELP CALM YOU.
AS YOU SLOWLY TRACE THE STARS BELOW, FOLLOW THE BREATHING
INSTRUCTIONS ON EACH OF THEIR LINES. REPEAT AS NEEDED!

R.I.P. OLD MIND-SETS

ON THE HEADSTONES, WRITE DOWN MIND-SETS YOU WOULD
LIKE TO RELEASE FROM YOUR LIFE, SUCH AS "JUDGING OTHERS,"
"DWELLING ON THE PAST," OR "RESISTING WHAT IS." YOU MIGHT
NOT BE ABLE TO CHANGE RIGHT NOW, BUT THIS IS A START!

YOU ALREADY
HAVE EVERYTHING
YOU NEED TO
SURVIVE THIS.

YOU HAVE YOU.

ANSWER KEY

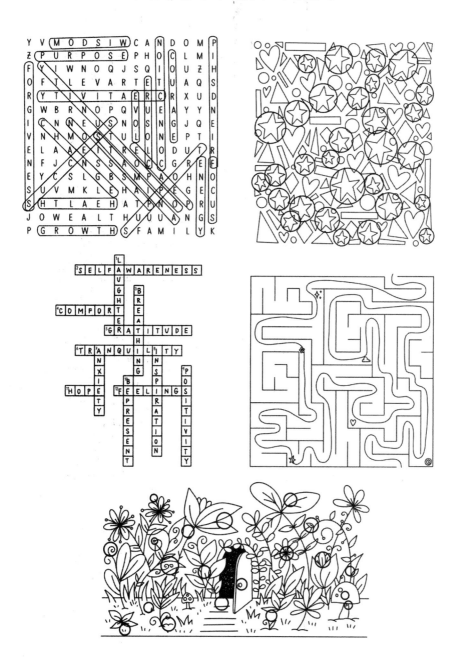

ACKNOWLEDGMENTS

THANK YOU TO EVERYONE WHO MADE THIS BOOK POSSIBLE!

TO MY FAMILY, THANK YOU FOR ALWAYS SUPPORTING MY IDEAS (AND DOING YOUR BEST TO UNDERSTAND MY ANXIETY!).

TO MY AGENT, MONIKA VERMA, THANK YOU FOR WADING WITH ME THROUGH ALL MY THOUGHTS AND PROVIDING THE KIND OF ENCOURAGEMENT THAT NEVER MAKES ME ANXIOUS TO EXPLORE NEW IDEAS.

TO MY EDITOR, LAUREN APPLETON, THANK YOU FOR GUIDING MY CREATIVITY AND TURNING IT FROM SQUIGGLES ON A SCREEN TO SOMETHING THAT ANXIOUS PEOPLE CAN HOLD ON TO.

TO MY FRIENDS, THANK YOU FOR BEING SO KIND AND COMPASSIONATE WHEN MY ANXIETY GETS IN THE WAY. YOU MATTER MORE THAN YOU KNOW.

ABOUT THE AUTHOR

DANI DIPIRRO IS AN (ANXIOUS!) AUTHOR AND ILLUSTRATOR LIVING IN A SUBURB OF WASHINGTON, DC. IN 2009, SHE CREATED THE WEBSITE POSITIVELYPRESENT.COM TO SHARE HER INSIGHTS ON TRYING TO LIVE A MORE POSITIVE, PRESENT LIFE.

DANI IS THE AUTHOR OF EVERYDAY OPTIMISM: HOW TO BE POSITIVE AND PRESENT AT WORK, AT HOME AND IN LOVE AND GROW THROUGH IT: INSPIRATION FOR WEATHERING LIFE'S SEASONS.

DANI SHARES HER WORK DAILY ON INSTAGRAM @POSITIVELYPRESENT. LEARN MORE ABOUT DANI AT POSITIVELYPRESENT.COM.